1001

BEST

THINGS
EVER SAID
ABOUT
HORSES

1001

BEST

THINGS
EVER SAID
ABOUT
HORSES

Edited by

Steven D. Price

THE LYONS PRESS
Guilford, Connecticut
An imprint of The Globe Pequot Press

The Lyons Press is an imprint of The Globe Pequot Press

10 9 8 7 6 5 4 3 2 1

Printed in the United States of America

Designed by Carol Sawyer/Rose Design

ISBN-13: 978-1-59228-983-7

ISBN-10: 1-59228-983-5

Library of Congress Cataloging-in-Publication data is available on file.

CONTENTS

INTRODUCTION

*I*t all began with one of the most clichéd quotations in the English language: "My kingdom for a horse!" My parents and I were out strolling through Central Park with relatives when a hansom cab rolled by, prompting my uncle to recite the line. "Hmm?" was my response. I was much younger then.

"Shakespeare," my uncle explained, and provided the context. What relevance an elderly draft-type animal plodding through a city park had to the desperate cry of the last Plantagenet monarch escaped me, but adults said and did strange things, and I didn't pursue the matter.

A few years later when the horse bug bit me and I started reading everything I could get my mitts on, I began to understand the magic that the printed horse world can work. The rhythms of "The Midnight Ride of Paul Revere" and "How They Brought the News From Aix to Ghent," the emotional impact of *Black Beauty* and *The Red*

Pony, and the excitement of *Ben-Hur* and *The Black Stallion* grabbed me the way they trapped every other horse-crazy kid.

With age and experience came an appreciation of wit (Churchill, Trollope, Twain, and Henny Youngman—surely the first time that comedian's name has appeared in the same sentence as the others) and wisdom, especially the literature of horsemanship from Xenophon and the Renaissance commentators to contemporaries Alois Podhadjsky, William Steinkraus, and Bill Dorrance.

That's why of my many book projects, compiling *The Quotable Horse Lover* was one of my very favorites, as rummaging through my library and picking the brains of like-minded friends and acquaintances meant revisiting old friends in print and making new ones.

That's also why I jumped at the chance to compile this book. More old friends, more new ones, and the opportunity to share them. Categories include—first and foremost—our love for horses, then the horse in literature, the horse in sport (a variety of disciplines and activities), riding and training (by which is meant riding and training in general and not for a specific sport), humor, and proverbs and other slices of wisdom.

Finding 1,001 entries sounded like a daunting task, but when the dust settled, I found that I had even more, which meant culling the herd.

Now, does that mean that these are indisputably *the* 1,001 best things ever said about horses? Not by a long shot, for there are indeed other equally wonderful quotations, but none, I daresay, might be considered better than the ones on these pages.

Although . . . earlier this year a very young rider stood at a horse show beside her not-much-taller pony. Her arms were around the pony's immaculately braided neck, and she was confiding something into one of its gray lop ears. The girl saw me watching and, with no reticence whatsoever, she volunteered that she was telling her pony that the mistake that happened in the last class was entirely her fault and certainly not his.

"He's a good pony, is he?" I asked.

"The best," she beamed. "I love him so much."

Ever the inquiring reporter, I asked why.

"Because he makes me feel happier than anything else does."

Others have tried to explain the effect that horses have on our lives, but has anyone said it any better?

Before exiting this arena, I tip my hat to the many people whose generous suggestions and contributions helped this project from start to finish, among whom are Don Burt, David Collins, Sue Copeland, Patti Ettinger, Norman Fine, Marnye Langer, Jenny Meyer, Judy Richter, Sally Stith, and Jim Wofford.

And a very special salute to my editor, colleague, and friend, Jessie Shiers.

STEVEN D. PRICE
NEW YORK, NEW YORK
AUGUST 2006

FOR THE
LOVE OF
HORSES

. . . For the [horse] shall not be measured by man. In a world older and more complete than ours they move finished and complete, gifted with extensions of the senses we have lost or never attained, living by voices we shall never hear. They are not brethren, they are not underlings; they are other nations caught with ourselves in the net of life and time, fellow prisoners of the splendour and travail of the earth.

—*Henry Beston*

They are more beautiful than anything in the world, kinetic sculptures, perfect form in motion.

—*Kate Millett*

In those border days every rider loved his horse as a part of himself. If there was a difference between any rider of the sage and Bostil, it was, as Bostil had more horses, so had he more love.

—*Zane Grey, "The Horses of Bostil's Ford"*

Horses are humanity's best friends. They have done everything for us, their friends. Think about war. Think about bad weather. Think about the Wild West in America. What would they have done without the horse?

—*George Theodorescu, in* Dressage Masters, *by David Collins*

For the wonderful brain of man
However mighty its force
Had never achieved its lordly plan
Without the aid of a horse.

—*Ella Wilcox*

Those who love horses are impelled by an ever-receding vision, some enchanted transformation through which the horse and the rider become a third, much greater thing.

—*Thomas McGuane, "Horses"*

What is a horse? It is freedom so indominable that it becomes useless to imprison it to serve man: it lets itself be domesticated, but with a simple, rebellious toss of the head—shaking its mane like an abundance of free-flowing hair—it shows that its inner nature is always wild, translucent and free.

—*Clarice Lispector, "Dry Point of Horses"*

There is moreover something magnificent, a kind of majesty in his whole frame, which exalts his rider with pride as he outstrips the wind in his course.

—*Paulus Jovius*

He must have a passion—not simply a liking—for horses, for nothing short of an absorbing passion can make him take the necessary interest in his mount. . . . The officer who never looks after his ponies after a game to see that they are properly put away; or who at the end of a long march or hard drill says, "Sergeant, fix up the horses, I'll be back soon," and then beats it, is not building for war; is not earning his pay. He is without pride and lazy, and the men know it and despise him while neglecting the horses.

—*George S. Patton, Jr.*

And here I say to parents, and especially to wealthy parents, Don't give your son money. As far as you can afford it, give him horses. No one ever came to grief—except honourable grief—through riding horses. No hour of life is lost that is spent in the saddle. Young men have often been ruined through owning horses, or through backing horses, but never through riding them; unless of course they break their necks, which, taken at a gallop, is a very good death to die.

—*Winston Churchill*

There on the tips of fair fresh flowers feedeth he; How joyous his neigh, . . . there in the midst of sacred pollen hidden, all hidden he; how joyous his neigh.

—*Navajo Song*

No one who longs for the "good old days" sighs for the passing of the working horse. Not if he or she loves horses.

—*Marion C. Garrety*

A lovely horse is always an experience. . . . It is an emotional experience of the kind that is spoiled by words.

—*Beryl Markham*

When God created the horse he said to the magnificent creature: I have made thee as no other. All the treasures of the earth lie between thy eyes. Thou shalt carry my friends upon thy back. Thy saddle shall be the seat of prayers to me. And thou fly without wings, and conquer without any sword.

—The Koran

The horse, the horse! The symbol of surging potency and power of movement, of action, in man.

—D. H. Lawrence

It makes men imperious to sit a horse.

—Oliver Wendell Holmes, Sr.

What delight to back the flying steed that challenges the wind for speed! . . . Whose soul is in his task, turns labour into sport!

—*James Sheridan Knowles*

I've come to realize that women and horses are fully capable of weaving new myths into the future, perspectives based not on conquest and domination, but on harmony and collaboration.

—*Linda Kohanov*, The Tao of Equus

Intimate acquaintance with the horse's knowledge and leading the kind of life that entails the continual reimaginings of horsemanship mark the faces of some older riders with the look that I have also seen on the faces of a few poets and thinkers, the incandescent gaze of unmediated awareness that one might be tempted to call innocence, since it is not unlike the gaze on the face of a child absorbed in Tinkertoys or a beautiful bug, but it is an achieved or restored innocence, and it is also terrible, the way Pasternak's face was terrible in its continuing steadiness of gaze.

—*Vicki Herne*, Adam's Task

But whether you regard the horse with awe or love, it is impossible to escape the sheer power of his presence, the phenomenal influence he exerts on the lives of all of us who decided at some stage that we wanted to become riders.

—*Mary Wanless*, The Natural Rider

I also belive that horses are the closest to God in the animal world. Horses are karmic, and they come to us in our lives karmicallly, when it is time for us truly to learn.

—*Dominique Barbier*, Dressage for the New Age

Whoever said a horse was dumb, was dumb.

—*Will Rogers*

If I was an artist like you, I would draw a true picture of Traveller; representing his fine proportions, muscular figure, deep chest, short back, strong haunches, flat legs, small head, broad forehead, delicate ears, quick eye, small feet, and black mane and tail. Such a picture would inspire a poet, whose genius could then depict his worth, and describe his endurance of toil, hunger, thirst, heat and cold; and the dangers and suffering through which he has passed. He could dilate upon his sagacity and affection, and his invariable response to every wish of his rider. He might even imagine his thoughts through the long night-marches and days of the battle through which he has passed. But I am no artist and can therefore only say he is a Confederate grey.

—Robert E. Lee, in a note to his wife's cousin who wished to paint a portrait of Lee's horse, Traveller

The sights and sounds of the countryside, as well as the color and action and excitement of the racecourse, are what turn me on: the mare suckling her foal, the renegade foal bothering all the others, the yearling who is boss of the field.

—Paul Mellon

Love means attention, which means looking after the things we love. We call this stable management.

—*George H. Morris*

In the saddle is heaven on earth.

—*Source unknown*

We are, in fact, a small army composed of slave masters who are in turn enslaved by our slaves. . . . We bathe, curry, brush, mane-pull, tail-detangle, hoof-pick, daub with salve, apply spray, and take off and put on blankets, fly sheets, leg wraps, bell boots. They stand there and loudly demand their food.

Yet, go into a stall, close the door. Wait a moment. Something will occur to you, something that seems to shift in the air between the two of you. It is the weight of power, the weightlessness of vulnerability, exchanging ions. The horse is there looking at you with eyes the color of chocolate pudding. He cannot escape you, or whatever it is you mean to do with him.

—*Melissa Pierson, "Personals"*

I am firmly convinced that if one squadron of horse cavalry and one pack troop of 200 mules had been available to me at San Stefano on August 1, they would have enabled me to cut off and capture the entire German force opposing me along the north coast road and would have permitted my entry into Messina at least forty-eight hours earlier.

—*Lt. General L.K. Truscot, Jr., during World War II*

Mounted units, schooled in American cavalry doctrine, would have been the perfect solution. Hardened and well trained horseman, possessing mobility and fire power, could have infiltrated through the extended German lines, encircled the delaying detachments, and would have permitted the maintenance of pressure on the retreating enemy main forces by our infantry division in their direct pursuit and would not have given the Germans sufficient time to prepare strong defensive positions to the north. As it was, there was no cavalry available.

—*Major General John P. Lucas, on the campaign
in southern Italy during World War II*

Wish I had a big fine horse,
and the corn to feed him on
I'd let little Shady Grove
feed him while I'm gone.

—Traditional Appalachian fiddle tune

My brother shall have a pair of horses with wings to fly among
the clouds.

—Rabindinrath Tagore, The Merchant

He has galloped through young girls' dreams, added richness to
grown women's lives, and served men in war and strife.

—Toni Robinson

A good horse knows just when to turn a cow, just how to cut a steer from the bunch. A good cow pony knows, as if by instinct, when to walk slowly through the brush, how to miss the gopher hole at a high canter. Many a cowboy owes his very life to his horse. The cowpoke and the cow pony become not just a team working in unison, they become as one.

—*Royal Hassrick*

A pony is a childhood dream, a horse is an adulthood treasure.

—*Rebecca Carroll*

A true horseman does not look at the horse with his eyes, he looks at his horse with his heart.

—*Source unknown*

He's the kind of horse with a far-away look. He'll sure take a man through some awful places and sometimes only one comes out.

—*Will James*

You and your horse. His strength and beauty. Your knowledge and patience and determination and understanding and love. That's what fuses the two of you into this marvelous partnership that makes you wonder. . . . What can heaven offer any better than what I have here on earth?

—*Monica Dickens*

I have seen things so beautiful they have brought tears to my eyes. Yet none of them can match the gracefulness and beauty of a horse running free.

—*Source unknown*

When your horse follows you without being asked, when he rubs his head on yours, and when you look at him and feel a tingle down your spine . . . you know you are loved.

—*John Lyons*

I am still under the impression there is nothing alive quite so beautiful as a thoroughbred horse.

—*John Galsworthy*

No heaven can heaven be, if my horse isn't there to welcome me.

—*Source unknown*

A dog may be man's best friend . . . but the horse wrote history.

—*Source unknown*

The Creator was glad. He had given habitations to his other creatures, forests to some, caves to others, but because of his enjoyment of the disinterested spirit of energy in the Horse, he gave him an open meadow under the eye of Heaven.

—*Rabindranath Tagore*

They say princes learn no art truly, but the art of horsemanship. The reason is, the brave beast is no flatterer. He will throw a prince as soon as his groom.

—*Ben Jonson*

It is the horse's gift to connect us with Heaven and our own footsteps.

—*Ronnie Sweet*

Horses are the dolphins of the plains, the spirits of the wind; yet we sit astride them for the sake of being well-groomed, whereas they could have all the desire in the world to bolt, but instead, they adjust their speed and grace, only to please us, never to displease.

—Lauren Salerno

We gaze upon their quiet beauty, their natural elegance, and we are captivated. They see us softly, in gentle light . . . rewarding human companionship with strength, grace and intelligence. As they run through arenas and open fields, past mountains and seas, moving like the wind toward heaven, we travel with them, if only in our hearts.

—Source unknown

Bread may feed my body, but my horse feeds my soul.

—*Source unknown*

Wherever man has left his footprint in the long ascent from
barbarism to civilization, we will find the hoofprint of a horse
beside it.

—*John Trotwood Moore*

I saw a child who couldn't walk, sit on a horse and laugh and talk. . . .
I saw a child who could only crawl, mount a horse and sit up tall. . . .
I saw a child born into strife, take up and hold the reins of life. . . .
And that same child was heard to say, thank you God for showing
me the way.

—*John Anthony Davis*

Look back on our struggle for freedom,
Trace our present day strength to its source,
And you'll find that man's pathway to glory,
Is strewn with the bones of a horse.

—Source unknown

Horse. . . . If God made anything more beautiful he kept it
for himself.

—Source unknown

The horses show him nobler powers;
O patient eyes, courageous hearts!

—Julian Grenfell, "Into Battle"

Horses show people that there are other wills and other consciences.
—Klaus Balkenhol, in Dressage Masters, *by David Collins*

Of all creatures God made at the Creation, there is none more
excellent, or so much to be respected as a horse.

—Bedouin legend

To see the wind's power, the rain's cleansing and the sun's radiant life,
one need only to look at the horse.

—Source unknown

Every single movement of Florian's revealed nobility, grace, signifi-
cance and distinction all in one; and in each of his poses he was the
ideal model for a sculptor, the composite of all the equestrian statues
in history.

—Felix Salten, "Florian"

All horses deserve, at least once in their lives, to be loved by
a little girl.

—Source unknown

You know horses are smarter than people. You never heard of a horse going broke betting on people.

—*Will Rogers*

Now the heart of a horse has love
For the master and home it knew:
And the mind of a horse can prove
That memory dwells there, too.

—*Ella Wheeler Wilcox*

Lo, the Turquoise Horse of Johano-ai . . .
There he spurns dust of glittering grain—
How joyous his neigh.

—*Navajo song of the horse*

As a young boy, I often dreamed of being a cavalry officer. How gallant and courageous these officers looked astride their prancing steeds as they paraded through the streets! How they seemed to be united as one being on the battlefield, an awesome force of courage, swiftness and power! Stronger than that image was the sense of partnership between these officers and their chargers, the incredible bond between them created by so many shared experiences and so many hours spent together.

—*Tad Coffin*

When we tell our stories about horses, they answer by telling us the truth, which can make for an unsettling transaction. . . . This isn't an equine moral posture, but a result of simply being horses. Of course horses can be wrong in their truthfulness—they may report a tiger in the laundry basket or a brace of dragons flying overhead—but this wrongness isn't deception. Horses do not lie.

—*Helen Husher*, Conversations with a Prince

Be not elated at any excellence that is not your own. If the horse in his elation were to say, "I am beautiful," it could be endured; but when you say in your elation, "I have a beautiful horse," rest assured that you are elated at something good that belongs to a horse.

—*Epictetus,* Discourses

I love the disciplined panic of a horse flirting with a tantrum at every turn, the delicate voluptuous play of muscles, the grace-sprung power.

—*Diane Ackerman*

It excites me that no matter how much machinery replaces the horse, the work it can do is still measured in horsepower . . . even in this space age. And although a riding horse often weighs half a ton, and a big drafter a full ton, either can be led about by a piece of string if he has been wisely trained. This to me is a constant source of wonder, and challenge.

—*Marguerite Henry*

. . . When I looked at life from the saddle and was as near to heaven as it was possible to be.

—Frances, Countess of Warwick, Discretions

The blood runs hot in the Thoroughbred and the courage runs deep. In the best of them, pride is limitless. This is their heritage and they carry it like a banner. What they have, they use.

—C. W. Anderson

The horse moved like a dancer, which is not surprising. A horse is a beautiful animal, but it is perhaps most remarkable because it moves as if it always hears music.

—Mark Helprin, A Winter's Tale

I heard a neigh, Oh, such a brisk and melodious neigh it was. My very heart leaped with the sound.

—*Nathaniel Hawthorne*

For the wonderful brain of man
However mighty its force
Had never achieved its lordly plan
Without the aid of a horse.

—*Ella Wilcox*

People, then, are not friend to horses unless their horses love them in return.

—*Plato*

Horse people may be heads of state or professionally unemployed in their private lives, but horses are their passion, as Jerusalem was the passion of a soldier in some ancient crusade. The cult of the horse as their idol is as central to their lives as cocaine is to some and applause is to others.

—Judith Krantz

A cowboy's best friend is his pony,
Yes sir I can prove it to you.
One day I was lost in a blizzard,
My pinto was faithful and true.

—Wilf Carter, "A Cowboy's Best Friend Is His Pony"

There is no way to tell non-horsey people that the companionship of a horse is not like that of a dog, or a cat, or a person. Perhaps the closest that two consciousnesses can ever come is the wordless simultaniety of horse and rider focusing together on a jump or a finish line or a canter pirouette, and then executing what they have intended together.

—Jane Smiley, "Mr. T's Heart"

People who have never lived on horseback and are not familiar with the big pastures in rough country would not understand the feeling that is developed among all members of a ranch family for certain individual horses. During this epidemic I rarely, if ever, heard discussed the value in dollars of a horse that was sick. The conversation about an older horse would concern the "good he had done" in helping establish a ranch or in helping raise the kids. In talking about one of the younger horses that were hard from constant use, the stories would be about the bad spots he had carried his rider though and how much endurance he had in rough country.

—*Ben K. Green*, The Village Horse Doctor

At the risk of sounding sexist—some wonderful trainers and handlers are male—I believe that women work best with horses in certain situations. I have seen a pigtailed ten-year-old girl quiet a raving 17-hand thoroughbred that had glimpsed out of the corner of his eye the vet's approach and was plunging around his stall in a full-scale tantrum. The youngster simply walked in, caught a piece of her friend's mane as he whirled past her, took a firm pinch hold on his neck skin, and slipped the halter over his nose before three male stable attendants with whips and twitches could agree on who was to undo the door latch.

—*Maxine Kumin, "Why Is It That Girls Love Horses?"*

The ability to control an animal so much bigger than herself gave her a sense of awe and wonderful power. It was, however, not only gratifying in a physical sense; the caring for, riding, and showing of the horse also represented the mastery of a world that was completely mysterious to the uninitiated.

—*John E. Schowalter, "Some Meanings of Being a Horsewoman"*

Our horses are our friends, companions, partners, teammates, and soulmates. They give us so much, so willingly—their strength, stamina, agility, and beauty—to give us the chance to vicariously experience the freedom and power that comes so naturally to them. When we accept the privilege of horse ownership, we must understand that we are taking on an enormous responsibility. Because we keep our horses locked in boxes or fenced in paddocks, we have taken away their ability to care for themselves as they do in the wild, roaming in search of food and water. They depend on us for their every need and desire. Therefore, we as horse owners carry a solemn responsibility to provide the best possible lives for our equine partners.

—*Jessie Shiers, 101 Horsekeeping Tips*

Oh, I am a Texas cowboy, as brave as I can be,
On my little Spanish pony I roam the wide prairie.
My trusty little pony is my companion true,
O'er creeks and hills and rivers he's sure to pull me through.

—*Traditional cowboy song, "The Jolly Cowboy"*

Horses are blessed with an alert expression, this despite the fact that they aren't half as smart as, say, a pig. Any halfway lonesome child who currycombs some rows in the dust caked on a horse's broad neck, or takes a minute to rub the white star on his forehead, is prompted by this look to feel that the horse loves and understands her as no one else. This myth is especially easy to fall into if the horse is steady and good-natured enough to take said kid on long rides without trying to scrape her off against a tree or otherwise showing fret over the burden of her.

—*Mary Karr,* The Liars' Club

In India, Prince Siddhartha, who was to become the Buddha, took great pride in his magnificent stallion Kanthaka. When he left his home, he called for his noble animal and spoke to him as a friend. "Today I go forth to seek supreme beatitude; lend me your help, O Kanthaka! Companions in arms or in pleasure are not hard to find, and we never want for friends when we set out to acquire wealth, but companions and friends desert us when it is the path of holiness we would take.

"Yet of this I am certain: he who helps another to do good or to do evil shares in that good or in that evil. Know then, O Kanthaka, that it is a virtuous impulse that moves me. Lend me your strength and your speed. The world's salvation and your own is at stake."

—*Buddhist legend*

The horse through all its trials has preserved the sweetness of paradise in its blood.

—*Johannes Jensen*

Let a horse whisper in your ear and breathe on your heart. You will never regret it.

—Source unknown

I love watching a good horse do what he's bred to do—I guess that's what I like the most about it. And I love to see good athletes do what they're bred to do.

—Wilford Brimley

If a poet knows more about a horse than he does about heaven, he might better stick to the horse, and some day the horse may carry him into heaven.

—Charles Ives

He was a horse of goodly countenance, rather expressive of vigilance than fire; though an unnatural appearance of fierceness was thrown into it by the loss of his ears, which had been cropped pretty close to his head.

—*Augustus B. Longstreet*

One must think when looking at a horse in motion, that it hears music inside its head.

—*Source unknown*

The eternal and wonderful sight of horses at liberty is magical to watch.

—*Bertrand Leclair*

Here is living harmony in horseflesh; an embodiment of rhythm and modulation, of point and counterpoint, that sang to the eye and made music in the heart.

—*John Hervey ("Salvadore"), on the great racehorse Equipoise*

Thou shall be for Man a source of happiness and wealth; thy back shall be a seat of honor, and thy belly of riches; every grain of barley given thee shall purchase indulgence for the sinner.

All the treasures of this earth lie between thine eyes. Thou shalt cast Mine enemies beneath thy hooves. . . . This shall be the seat from whence prayers rise unto me.

—*The Koran*

Machinery may make for efficiency and a standardisation of life, but horse love is a bond of freemasonry which unites the entire race. . . .

—*William Fawcett*

There comes a point in every rider's life when he wonders if it's all worth it. Then one look at the horse, and he realizes—it is.

—*Kelly Stewart*

A bad ride is much better than a good walk.

—*Peter Grace*

Jess stopped laughing but said nothing. He figured Eliza had gone about as far in one day as a woman could in enlarging her appreciation of horseflesh; still he couldn't help smiling when he thought of the sermon that might have been preached in the Bethel Church upon eternal verities.

—*Jessamyn West*, Friendly Persuasion

He was as near living flame as horses ever get.

—*Joe Palmer, on Man O'War*

He will be your children's playmate; a child himself, he'll do no harm. He'll pardon like no other your omissions, errors, thoughtless handling. His back, a throne of feathers, will bear you smoothly at the trot and gallop. He'll go where others dare not. He'll stand firm where others flee in terror. You'll discover that the pirouette is easy, that a rein back can go on forever, that you need not be a great rider to perform airs above the ground. At the spur's light touch he'll take flight with the wind, bearing you safely through the air laden with long forgotten fragrance. With him, the distant mountains will be clearer, brighter the light of the stars, the trilling of the nightingale more joyful, sweeter the gurgling of the streams. And at last you'll understand why he was e'er the chosen one of kings.

—*Juan Llamas on the Andalusian horse*

Stay away from a horse long enough and you'll start tapping your fingers to the beat of a trot.

—*Source unknown*

When you are on a great horse, you have the best seat you will
ever have.

—Sir Winston Churchill

Nothing is more sacred as the bond between horse and rider . . . no
other creature can ever become so emotionally close to a human as a
horse. When a horse dies, the memory lives on because an enormous
part of his owner's heart, soul, very existence dies also . . . but that
can never be laid to rest, it is not meant to be. . . .

—Stephanie M. Thorn

Eager as fire though the last goal is won,
These wilding creatures gentled to the rein,
These little brothers of the wind and sun.

—Eleanor Baldwin, "Polo Ponies"

Wherever thrumming hoofbeats drum
As galloping riders go or come;
Wherever a saddle is still a throne
And dust of hoofs by wind is blown;
Wherever are horsemen, young or old,
The Pacing Mustangs's tale is told.

—*Anonymous poet, "The White Mustang"*

We attended stables, as we attended church, in our best clothes, no doubt showing the degree of respect due to horses, no less than to the deity.

—*Sir Osbert Sitwell*

Closeness, friendship, affection: keeping your own horse means all these things.

—*Bertrand Leclair*

Of all animals kept for the recreation of mankind the horse is alone capable of exciting a passion that shall be absolutely hopeless.

—*Bret Harte*

When one is on horseback he knows all things.

—*George Herbert*

In riding a horse, we borrow freedom.

—*Pam Brown*

The connection between people and horses is both ancient and timeless. Even as equestrian sports and disciplines change and grow, the tie remains secure.

—*Eliza McGraw*

To many, the words love, hope, and dreams are synonymous with horses.

—Oliver Wendell Holmes

Some people object to high-blowers, that is, 'osses wot make a noise like steam-engines as they go. I don't see no great objection to them myself, and think the use they are of clearin' the way in crowded thoroughfares, and the protection they afford in dark night by preventin' people ridin' against you, more than counterbalance any disconvenience.

—Robert Smith Surtees (John Jorrock), Handley Cross

As a boy in a prairie town I learned early to revere the work horse. To me, as to all boys, a dog was a slave, but a horse was a hero. And the men who handled him were heroes too.

—James Stevens, Horses

His neck is high and erect, his head replete with intelligence, his belly short, his back full, and his proud chest swells with hard muscles.

—*Virgil*, Georgics (*III*, 79)

The horse is a creature who sacrifices his own being to exist through the will of another . . . he is the noblest conquest of man.

—*George Louis Leclerc, Comte de Buffon*

I ride because I rode as a child when life was simpler and somehow more complete. Only the whiff of a clean horse is needed to remind [me] of days gone by. For always there have been the horses.

I ride because of all the great horse souls who have shared their lives with me and taught me more than I can say. Their names and faces flash before me as old friends. I ride because of all the horses I shall never ride. Those I have watched and marveled at from afar for all their grace and beauty. This the stuff of a child's dream, the kind that doesn't die with time. Always there are the horses.

I ride because the seasons call to me. Each unique in its appeal and all quite frequently best viewed from the back of a favorite horse. I ride because of all things, horses are my passion. They inspire and encourage, energize, and challenge in ways I cannot explain to the un-initiated. I ride because of the rush of stretching one's self just a bit farther today than before both mind and body. Always there are the horses.

I ride because of those briefest of spans when the partnership comes to full promise. When the path twists and barriers fall, each footfall is measured and balanced between the two as a dance. There are no others . . . only this moment and this single step to ride. The memories of those times stand vivid in my mind to be recalled with all the freshness of the day at will and in times less grand.

But if I must choose, I ride because I have dreams yet to live. I ride because I have dreams yet to have and what exactly they will be tomorrow I cannot say . . . but always there will be the horses.

—*Author unknown, "Always There Are the Horses"*

The nature of the horse remains unchanged, whether it carries the saddle of the prince, or whether it draws the cart of the wagoner. The noble ones accept the yoke, they serve, but will never be slaves, for to themselves they can never be traitors.

—H. H. Isenbart

Silence takes on a new quality when the only sound is that of regular and smooth hoof beats.

—Bertrand Leclair

Despite the unique all-around athleticism of the horse, "keeping on keeping on" is what most horses do best. This has been true over the whole 10,000-plus years that man and horse have cooperated to shape human destiny and global change. But this gift of wings to the rider obliges mankind, in return, to be the steward of the horse, to respect and meet his needs from birth through death, at work and rest, in health and decline.

—Matthew Mackay-Smith, in Marnye Langer's The Tevis Cup

One of the sayings in the horse world is that a clean horse is a happy horse, but in my experience this is not really true. Horses like dirt, and go to considerable trouble to burrow around in as much of it as they can find. But what horses do like is to be tended, and I think this is what this old saw points to—being touched and noticed and having their parts inspected and admired puts them in a good mood. Some horses will tell you they don't like it by twitching and rolling their eyes and making objections, but this is usually because they don't like being worked, and horses tend to be groomed right before they are ridden. This contaminates what ought to be a pleasant interaction for everybody.

—*Helen Husher*, Conversations with a Prince

Enthusiasm for horses cuts across generations. A Midwestern boy learns from his grandfather how to train draft horses for county fair weight-pulling contests. Young girls have schoolroom daydreams about blue ribbons until it is time to race to local stables and favorite mounts. Suburban housewives sandwich an hour's hacking between carpools and shopping trips, and when dinner talk turns to riding, they and their children pursuade Daddy to try. He does, likes it in spite of stiff muscles, and joins several commuter pals in an evening instruction class at the stable.

—*Steven D. Price*, Panorama of American Horses

[Thoroughbreds] are exuberant. They are sensitive. They have opinions. They in general have too much of every lively quality than too little.

—*Jane Smiley*

We horsemen live in a little world by ourselves. We live, breathe and dream horses. We become so wrapped up in horses that we do not understand why everyone cannot understand us.

—*P. T. Albert*

To live without horses is to carry them with you always.

—*Maxine Kumin*

As I browse through my field in Virginia
And muse, at the close of the day
Once again they will give me a medal
Made of silver, although it ain't hay.

—*Paul Mellon [imagining the appreciation
of one of his horses that won a prize]*

There will always be stock horses. When all our needs can finally be fulfilled by merely pressing a button, there will still be men who ride horses to bring the cows to market.

—*Paul T. Albert, founding editor of* Western Horseman

We may fly or sail or glide over the roads on pneumatic tires with more comfort, but the love of good horseflesh will never be stamped out of humans while they still have red blood in their veins. This is not a prophesy, but a fact.

—*Paul T. Albert*

The hooves of a horse! Oh! Witching and sweet is the music earth
steals from the iron-shod feet; no whisper of love, no trilling of bird,
can stir me as hooves of the horse have stirred.

—*Will H. Ogilvie*

If a man sweats while doing a job horseback, that's somehow
romantic; if the same man soils his hands afoot, he's nothing more
than a common laborer.

—*Kurt Markus*

After seeing kids play polo against big guys, it only shows that horses
are the greatest equalizer in the world. No matter what you weigh,
the little fellow is your equal on a horse.

—*Will Rogers*

Hundreds and hundreds of beautiful horses in the [Santa Barbara] parade, and a man without a silver saddle is a vagrant.

—*Will Rogers*

A man that don't love a horse, there is something the matter with him. If he has no sympathy for the man that does love horses then there is something worse the matter with him.

—*Will Rogers*

Every day I pray to God to give me horses—wonderful horses—to make me the best rider in England.

—*Velvet Brown, in* National Velvet, *by Enid Bagnold*

I can't help it, Father. I'd sooner have that horse happy than go
to heaven.

> —*Velvet Brown, in* National Velvet, *by Enid Bagnold*

His nature just speaks to me. I didn't want him too far back to get dirt
in his face, to get discouraged.

> —*Julie Krone (b. 1963), U.S. jockey describing her "mystical
> relationship" with Colonial Affair, the horse that she rode to
> the first-ever victory by a woman jockey in a prestigious
> Triple Crown race: the Belmont Stakes on June 5, 1993.*

Never let his fire die out, but kindle it with words. Let him know
that you are honored to be carried along on his strong shoulders
and swift feet.

> —*Carl Raswan*

The horse is an archetypal symbol which will always find ways to stir up deep and moving ancestral memories in every human being

—*Paul Mellon*

When life hands me lemons, I don't make lemonade, I go for a ride; horses are my family.

—*Judy Richter*

Far back, far back in our dark soul the horse prances.

—*D. H. Lawrence*

Here lies the body of my good horse, The General. For years he bore me around the circuit of my practice and all that time he never made a blunder. Would that his master could say the same.

—*John Tyler's epitaph for his horse*

If I had a horse, I'd ride off in the sunset, where dreams, and shadows lie. To a life, where pain and sorrow don't exist, and to where hopes, and dreams become reality.

—Lindsay Turcotte

It is wonderful when one is out with these animals, how attached they become. There are times when I would walk up to my horse, that he would nicker in a low tone and run his nose against me in a very knowing manner.

—H.S. Young

You can tell a horse owner by the interior of their car. Boots, mud, pony nuts, straw, items of tack and a screwed-up waxed jacket of incredible antiquity. There is normally a top layer of children and dogs.

—Helen Thompson

My horses are my friends, not my slaves.

—*Reiner Klimke*

As a horse runs, think of it as a game of tag with the wind.

—*Tre Tuberville*

A horse is the projection of peoples' dreams about themselves—strong, powerful, beautiful—and it has the capability of giving us escape from our mundane existence.

—*Pam Brown*

When will they make a tractor that can furnish the manure for farm fields and produce a baby tractor every spring?

—*George Rupp, pioneer breeder of Belgian horses*

To me, horses and freedom are synonymous.

—Veryl Goodnight

A good rider on a good horse is as much above himself and others as the world can make him.

—Lord Herbert

Take most people, they're crazy about cars. I'd rather have a goddam horse. A horse is at least human, for godsake.

—J. D. Salinger, Catcher in the Rye

. . . he did not feel the ground under his feet . . . he thrust himself into the capriole, rose high in the air . . . forelegs and hindlegs horizontal. He soared above the ground, his head high in jubilation. Conquering!

—Felix Salten, "Florian"

My horse has a hoof of striped agate; His fetlock is like fine eagle plume. His legs are like quick lightening. My horse has a tail like a trailing black cloud. His mane is made of short rainbows. My horse's eyes are made of big stars.

—*Navajo war god's horse song*

Wherever man has left his footprint in the long ascent from barbarism to civilization we will find the hoofprint of the horse beside it.

—*John Trotwood Moore*

If you have it, it is for life. It is a disease for which there is no cure. You will go on riding even after they have to haul you on a comfortable wise old cob, with feet like inverted buckets and a back like a fireside chair . . . when I can't ride anymore, I shall still keep horses as long as I can hobble about with a bucket and a wheelbarrow. When I can't hobble, I shall roll my wheelchair out to the fence of the field where my horses graze, and watch them.

—*Monica Dickens*

Through the days of love and celebration and joy, and through the
dark days of mourning—the faithful horse has been with us always.

—*Elizabeth Cotton*

... This most noble beast is the most beautiful, the swiftest and
of the highest courage of domesticated animals. His long mane and
tail adorn and beautify him. He is of a fiery temperament, but good
tempered, obedient, docile and well-mannered.

—*Pedro Garcia Conde*

Horses do change, you know; a lot of the . . . ponies really give the
able-bodied grooms a hard time, but if you put a disabled child or
adult on their back they're as gentle as lambs. I don't know what it is:
they seem to sense something.

—*Jackie Croome*

A horse can lend its rider the speed and strength he or she lacks—but the rider who is wise remembers it is no more than a loan.

—*Pam Brown*

The farmer's horse is never lame, never unfit to go. Never throws out curbs, never breaks down before or behind. Like his master he is never showy. He does not paw and prance, and arch his neck, and bid the world admire his beauties . . . and when he is wanted, he can always do his work.

—*Anthony Trollope*

I'm kind of sorry now so many were caught, 'cause I have a lot of respect and admiration for the mustang. The fact that he'd give us back the same medicine we'd hand him, with sometimes a little overdose, only made me feel that in him, I had an opponent worthy of the game. Even though I'd get sore at them when they'd put it over on us and rub it in a little too hard, the satisfaction I'd get at catching some wise bunch didn't last very long when I'd remember they'd be shipped, put to work and maybe starved into being good by some hombre who was afraid of them and didn't savvy at all. For they really belong, not to man, but to that country of junipers and sage, of deep arroyos, mesas—and freedom.

> —*Will James, cowboy and author,*
> *about his earlier days as a horse hunter*

A man on a horse is spiritually as well as physically bigger than a man on foot.

> —*John Steinbeck*

Many people have sighed for the "good old days" and regretted the "passing of the horse," but today, when only those who like horses own them, it is a far better time for horses.

—*C. W. Anderson*

Horses change lives. They give our young people confidence and self-esteem. They provide peace and tranquillity to troubled souls— they give us hope.

—*Toni Robinson*

The sight of him did something to me I've never quite been able to explain. He was more than tremendous strength and speed and beauty of motion. He set me dreaming.

—Walt Morey

The substitution of the internal combustion engine for the horse marked a very gloomy milestone in the progress of mankind.

—*Sir Winston Churchill*

~

Most important is love of the horse. It is the leitmotif that should underlie all our intercourse with the most lovable of creatures. A horse will overcome its inborn shyness and gain confidence, the fundamental condition for mutual understanding, with a man whose love it feels. Subsequently, when strictness or punishment becomes necessary, the horse will know that it was deserved, for it has never suffered injustice or arbitrariness.

—*Waldemar Seunig, "Horsemanship"*

~

A canter is a cure for every evil.

—*Benjamin Disraeli*

~

There is something about riding down the street on a prancing horse
that makes you feel like something, even when you ain't a thing.

—*Will Rogers*

When they lay me down to rest
Put my spurs and rope upon my chest
Get my friends to carry me
and then go turn my horses free.

—*Epitaph for Clyde Kennedy*

Ain't nuthin' like ridin' a fine horse in new country.

—*Augustus MacCrae, in* Lonesome Dove

The most beautiful, the most spirited and the most inspiring creature
ever to print foot on the grasses of America.

—*J. Frank Dobie, on the mustang*

A man, a horse and a dog never get weary of each other's company.

—*Source unknown*

Of all the animals the horse is the best friend of the Indian, for without it he could not go on long journeys. A horse is the Indian's most valuable piece of property. If an Indian wishes to gain something, he promises that if the horse will help him he will paint it with native dye, that all may see that help has come to him through the aid of his horse.

—*Brave Buffalo, late nineteenth-century Teton Sioux medicine man*

. . . there's nothin' in life that's worth doin', if it cain't be done from a horse . . .

—*Red Steagall, "Born to This Land"*

By reason of his elegance, he resembles an image painted in a palace, though he is as majestic as the palace itself.

—Emir Abd-el-Kader

Riding a horse is not a gentle hobby, to be picked up and laid down like a game of Solitaire. It is a grand passion.

—Ralph Waldo Emerson

A horse is the projection of peoples' dreams about themselves—strong, powerful, beautiful—and it has the capability of giving us escape from our mundane existence.

—Pam Brown

People on horses look better than they are. People in cars look worse than they are.

—*Myra Mannes*

There is something about the outside of a horse that is good for the inside of a man.

—*Sir Winston Churchill*

There is no secret so close as that between a rider and his horse.

—*R. S. Surtees*

The wind flew. God told to wind to condense itself and out of the flurry came the horse. But with the spark of sprit the horse flew by the wind itself.

—*Margarite Henry*, King of the Wind

We have almost forgotten how strange a thing it is that so huge and powerful and intelligent an animal as a horse should allow another, and far more feeble animal, to ride upon its back.

—Peter Gray

Horses make a landscape look beautiful.

—Alice Walker

I sit astride life like a bad rider on a horse. I only owe it to the horse's good nature that I am not thrown off at this very moment.

—Ludwig Wittgenstein, Austrian philosopher

Again the early-morning sun was generous with its warmth. All the sounds dear to a horseman were around me—the snort of the horses as they cleared their throats, the gentle swish of their tails, the tinkle of irons as we flung the saddles over their backs—little sounds of no importance, but they stay in the unconscious library of memory.

—Wynford Vaughan-Thomas

The horsey life is an unending journey to the limits of the human mind. It is an attempt to understand, not an alien culture or an alien religion or an alien race, but an alien species. The extraordinary and thrilling affinity between the radically different minds of humans and horses has rewarded both humans and horses for thousands of years.

Even in the twenty-first century, we turn to horses. No, let me rephrase that. Especially in the twenty-first century, we turn to horses. Our world is too tame, too comfortable, and our children grow up in shopping malls with childhoods circumscribed by paedophilia-phobia and the laws on health and safety. We are becoming a species cut off from all others, and it doesn't feel good.

But when we associate with horses, we claim back something of our lost wildness, our lost wilderness. With horses, we are back in touch with our fellow animals. With horses, we become more truly human.

—Simon Barnes

Horses and dogs have been man's most intimate and faithful companions since the dawn of history, but the horse has certainly been the most useful. In sport, agriculture, transport and warfare, the horse has contributed more to human pleasure, ambition and progress than any other animal.

—Prince Philip, Duke of Edinburgh

A horse loves freedom, and the weariest old work horse will roll on the ground or break into a lumbering gallop when he is turned loose into the open.

—Gerald Raferty

The child who ran weeping to you with a cut finger is now brought home, smiling gamely, with a broken collar bone and incredible contusions. "It wasn't Jezebel's fault Dad."

—Pam Brown

We have been companions now for centuries. I rode you in the high festival to the Parthenon and to the edges of the unknown world under the Shadow of the Eagles. Together we re-took the Holy Places, endured the horrors of the crossing to Crimea. You took me to adventure and to love. We two have shared great joy and great sorrow. And now I stand at the gate of the paddock watching you run in an ecstasy of freedom, knowing you will return to stand quietly, loyally beside me.

—*Pam Brown*

Where in this world can man find nobility without pride, friendship without envy, beauty without vanity? Here, where grace is laced with muscle, and strength by gentleness confined. He serves without servility; he has fought without enmity. There is nothing so powerful, nothing less violent; there is nothing so quick, nothing more patient. England's past has been borne on his back. All our history is his industry. We are his heirs, he is our inheritance. Ladies & Gentlemen —the Horse!

—*Ronald Duncan*

Since the dawn of civilization, the horse and the Muses have been boon companions in all the heroics of mythology and history.

—*Robert Frothingham*

One of the earliest religious disappointments in a young girl's life devolves upon her unanswered prayer for a horse.

—*Phyllis Theroux*

The rhythm of the ride carried them on and on, and she knew that the horse was as eager as she, as much in love with the speed and air and freedom.

—*Georgess McHargue*

You know you love your horse when your mouth waters at the sight of a wagon-full of hay.

—*Source unknown*

Honor lies in the mane of a horse.

—*Herman Melville*

The white horse moved like a dancer, which is not surprising: a horse is a beautiful animal, but it is perhaps most remarkable because it moves as if it always hears music.

—*Mark Helprin*, A Winter's Tale

There is a touch of divinity even in brutes, and a special halo about a horse that should forever exempt him from indignities.

—*Herman Melville*

His hooves pound the beat, your heart sings the song.

—*Jerry Shulman*

There are many wonderful places in the world, but one of my favourite places is on the back of my horse.

—*Rolf Kopfle*

The freedom of riding horseback has a place all its own; the companionship of a horse means you'll never be alone.

—*Herman Geithoom*

Yet when the books have been read and reread, it boils down to the horse, his human companion, and what goes on between them. Many professional horsemen scoff at anything that resembles a sentimental relationship between horse and rider. Yet I have heard these same men admit countless times that horses perform better for some people than others. They're apt to attribute it to anything but what I think it is—love.

—*Walter Farley, author of* The Black Stallion *series*

I never encountered a horse in whose soul there was no harmony to call on.

—*Vicki Hearne*

For never man had friend
More enduring to the end,
Truer mate in every turn of time and tide.
Could I think we'd meet again
It would lighten half my pain?
At the place where the old horse died.

—*G. J. Whyte-Melville,*
"The Place Where the Old Horse Died"

To thee, my master, I offer my prayer.

Treat me as a living being, not as a machine.

Feed me, water and care for me, and when the day's work is done, groom me carefully so that my circulation may act well, for remember: a good grooming is equivalent to half a feed. Clean my feet and legs and keep them in good condition, for they are the most important parts of my body.

Pet me sometimes, be always gentle to me so that I may serve you the more gladly and learn to love you.

Do not jerk the reins, do not whip me when I am going uphill. Do not force me out of the regular gait or you will not have my strength when you want it. Never strike, beat or kick me when I do not understand what you mean, but give me a chance to understand you. Watch me, and if I fail to do your bidding, see if something is not wrong with my harness or feet.

Don't draw the straps too tight: give me freedom to move my head. Don't make my load too heavy, and oh! I pray thee, have me well shod every month.

Examine my teeth when I do not eat; I may have some teeth too long or I may have an ulcerated tooth and that, you know, is very painful. Do not tie my head in an unnatural position or take away my best defense against flies and mosquitoes by cutting off my tail.

I cannot, alas, tell you when I am thirsty, so give me pure, cold water frequently. Do all you can to protect me from the sun; and throw a cover over me—not when I am working, but when I am standing in the cold.

I always try to do cheerfully the work you require of me: and day and night I stand for hours patiently waiting for you.

In this war, like any other soldier, I will do my best without hope of any war-cross, content to serve my country and you, and, if need be, I will die calm and dignified on the battlefield; therefore, oh! my master, treat me in the kindest way and your God will reward you here and hereafter.

I am not irreverent if I ask this, my prayer, in the name of Him who was born in a stable.

—"The Artillery Horse's Prayer," by Captain De Condenbove, French Army, during World War I

It must be confessed that horses at present work too exclusively for men, rarely men for horses; and the brute degenerates in man's society.

—Henry David Thoreau

Horses and children, I often think, have a lot of the good sense there is in the world.

—Josephine Demott Robinson, U.S. circus performer,
The Circus Lady

~

Horses are predictably unpredictable

—Loretta Gage

~

There is something about jumping a horse over a fence, something that makes you feel good. Perhaps it's the risk, the gamble. In any event it's a thing I need.

—William Faulkner

~

A cowboy is a man with guts and a horse.

—Will James

~

Riding turns "I wish" into "I can."

—*Pam Brown*

You can tell a true cowboy by the type of horse that he rides

—*Cowboy expression*

A good man will take care of his horses and dogs, not only while they are young, but also when they are old and past service.

—*Plutarch*

"He's not going to look back if you don't," he said, "They're the most forgiving creatures God ever made."

—*Nicolas Evans*, The Horse Whisperer

There is a secret pleasing and cherishing of the horse with the bridle, which the rider must accomplish with so unperceiving a motion that none but the beast may know it.

—*Gervaise Markham*

Content with harmless sport and simple food,
Boundless in faith and love and gratitude;
Happy the man, if there be any such—
Of whom his epitaph can say as much.

—*Lord Sherbrooke, "A Horse's Epitaph"*

No honors wait him, medal, badge or star,
Though scarce could war a kindlier deed unfold;
He bears within his breast, more precious far
Beyond the gift of kings, a heart of gold.

—*Anonymous, "Goodbye, Old Friend," inspired by an incident on the road to a battery position in Flanders during World War I*

What are we, we your horses,
So loyal where we serve,
Fashioned of noble forces
All sensitive with nerve?
Torn, agonized, we wallow
On the blood-bemired sod;
And still the shiploads follow.
Have horses then no God?
> —*Katherine Lee Bates,* "The Horses" *[the poem begins with a headnote:* "Thus far 80,000 horses have been shipped from the United States to the European belligerants"]

I pray the gentle hands may guide my feet;
I ask for kind commands from voices sweet;
At night a stable warm with scented hay,
Where, safe from every harm, I'll sleep till day.
> —*Anonymous,* "A Pony's Prayer"

THE HORSE'S PRAYER

I'm only a horse, dear Master, but my heart is warm and true,
And I'm ready to work my hardest, for the pleasure of pleasing you.
Good corn, and hay, and water, are all that I wish to ask.
And a warm dry bed to rest on, when I've finished my daily task.
Don't strike me in needless anger if I'm slow to understand,
But encourage my drooping spirits with a gentle voice and hand.
Finally, O my master! When my health and strength are gone,
When I'm getting old and feeble, and my long life's work is done,
Don't sell me to cruel owners, to be slaved to my latest breath,
But grant me the untold blessing of a quick and painless death;
That, as you have always found me a patient and loyal friend,
The years of my faithful service may be crowned by a peaceful end.
I plead in the name of the Savior, Who cares when the sparrows fall.
Who was born in a lowly stable, and knows, and loves us all!

—*Anonymous, "The Horse's Prayer"*

II

HORSE LAUGHS

On horseback he seemed to require as many hands as a Hindu god, at least four for clutching the reins, and two more for patting the horse soothingly on the neck.

—*H. H. Munro ("Saki")*

I never play horseshoes 'cause Mother taught us not to throw our clothes around.

—*"Mr. Ed" [the "talking horse" of the 1970s TV series]*

[He was] so learned that he could name a horse in nine languages. . . . So ignorant that he bought a cow to ride on.

—*Benjamin Franklin*

[Robert Frost] was like a horse you could get along with if you came up beside him on the okay side.

—*Archibald MacLeisch*

There are no handles to a horse, but the 1910 model has a string to each side of its face for turning its head when there is something you want it to see.

—Stephen Leacock, "Reflections on Riding"

The one thing I do not want to be called is First Lady. It sounds like a saddle horse.

—Jacqueline Kennedy Onassis

Life ain't certain . . . ride your best horse first.

—Source unknown

Upon the Virtues of the Horse?
They are too numerous to tell
Save when you have a Horse to Sell.

—Henry Wheeler Shaw, Josh Billings: His Sayings

I saw him out riding in the Row, clutching to his horse like a string of onions.

—*Margot Asquith*

MUSTANG, n. An indocile horse of the western plains. In English society, the American wife of an English nobleman.

—*Ambrose Bierce*, The Devil's Dictionary

Oh wasn't it naughty of Smudges?
Oh, Mummy, I'm sick with disgust.
She threw me in front of the Judges,
And my silly old collarbone's bust.

—*John Bettjeman, "Hunter Trials"*

I hope I break even, I need the money.

—*Joe E. Lewis [on betting]*

Racetrack humor from Henny Youngman:

⁀ I played a great horse yesterday! It took seven horses to beat him.

⁀ The horse I bet on was so slow, the jockey kept a diary of the trip.

⁀ My horse's jockey was hitting the horse. The horse turns around and says "Why are you hitting me, there is nobody behind us!"

⁀ That was the first time I saw a horse start from a kneeling position!

⁀ My horse was so late getting home, he tiptoed into the stable.

⁀ I don't mind when my horse is left at the post. I don't mind when my horse comes up to me in the stands and asks "Which way do I go?" But when the horse I bet on is at the $2 window betting on another horse in the same race . . .

I may mention that my experience of riding has thrown a very
interesting sidelight upon a rather puzzling point in history. It is
recorded of the famous Henry the Second that he was "almost
constantly in the saddle, and of so restless a disposition that he never
sat down, even at meals." I had hitherto been unable to understand
Henry's idea about his meals, but I think I can appreciate it now.

—*Stephen Leacock*, Reflections on Riding

Ascot is so exclusive that it is the only racecourse in the world where
the horses own the people.

—*Art Buchwald*

'Orses and dorgs is some men's fancy. They're wittles and drink
to me.

—*Charles Dickens*, David Copperfield

In Westerns you were permitted to kiss your horse but never
your girl.

—*Gary Cooper, U.S. screen actor*

They say he rides as if he's part of the horse, but they don't say
which part.

—*Robert Sherwood, reviewing cowboy hero Tom Mix*

Vivian Rutledge: Speaking of horses, I like to play them myself. I like to see them work out a little first. See if they're front runners or come from behind.

Philip Marlowe: Find out mine?

Vivian Rutledge: I think so.

Philip Marlowe: Go ahead.

Vivian Rutledge: I'd say you don't like to be rated. You like to get in front, open up a lead, take a little breather in the back stretch, and, then, come home free.

Philip Marlowe: You don't like to be rated yourself.

Vivian Rutledge: I haven't met anyone yet that could do it. Any suggestions?

Philip Marlowe: I can't tell till I've seen you over a distance of ground. You've got a touch of class, but I don't know how . . . how far you can go.

Vivian Rutledge: A lot depends on who's in the saddle.

—The Big Sleep, *screenplay by William Faulkner, Leigh Brackett, Jules Furthmann, and Howard Hawks*

And if you please, one that can show . . . just locally of course,
Perhaps a little Medal/Maclay or equitation horse.
Of course, I really wouldn't mind if I found out that you had sent
A horse to hunt and show and hack and perhaps three-day event.

—*Cooky McClung*

A man from Idaho who breezed into a Kentucky racetrack with an unraced six-year-old horse. The horse won his maiden race easily and paid a whopping price.

The racing stewards didn't like the look of the thing and questioned the owner. "Is this horse unsound?" they asked.

"Not a bit," said the owner.

"In that case," asked one of the stewards, "why haven't you ever raced him before?"

"Mister," said the man from Idaho, "we couldn't even catch the critter until he was five years old."

—*Joe Palmer*

I realize that the concept of wild horses probably stirs romantic notions in many of you, but this is because you have never met any wild horses in person. In person, they are like enormous hooved rats. They amble up to your camp site, and their attitude is: "We're wild horses. We're going to eat your food, knock down your tent and poop on your shoes. We're protected by federal law, just like Richard Nixon."

—*Dave Barry*

Does it really matter what these affectionate people do—so long as they don't do it in the streets and frighten the horses!

—*Mrs. Patrick Campbell*

One had to be more in command, so to speak, upon a horse than on a boat deck. There was no first mate to give orders to if the horse happened to drift in the wrong direction. Also, the man pointed out after having done it several times, if he fell off a horse it hurt a lot more hitting the ground than if he fell off the boat and hit the water. Also, nine times out of ten, the horse would not wait for him to get back aboard. Neither, insisted his bride, would a boat, only a horse didn't go all the way to England if turned loose.

—*Cooky McClung, "From Sailboats
to Snaffles in One Easy Marriage"*

Certain comic effects can be achieved by a brand-new rider, especially a man who dresses like a fashion model and rides like a tailor.

—*C. J. J. Mullen*

Never approach a bull from the front, a horse from the rear, or a fool from any direction.

—*Cowboy humor*

CENTAUR: One of a race of persons who lived before the division of labor had been carried to such a pitch of differentiation, and who followed the primitive economic maxim, "every man his own horse."

—*Ambrose Bierce*, The Devil's Dictionary

The first time I went horseback riding, I climbed on the horse and everything was going fine until the horse started bouncing out of control. I tried with all my might to hang on, but I was thrown off. Just when things could not possibly get worse, my foot got caught in the stirrup as I fell head first to the ground.

The horse kept going, and my head continued to bounce harder as the horse did not stop or even slow down. Just as I was giving up hope and losing consciousness, the Wal*Mart manager ran out and unplugged the machine.

Thank heaven for heroes!

—*Source unknown*

Electronic transfer of funds.

—*Walter T. Kees, when asked for the best thing ever said about horses*

Don't know what to do to-day,
There's my fine new rocking-horse,
Long of tail and dapple-gray,
I *might* ride on him of course:
But my new velocipede—
What would *it* do then? or what
Would that "fiery, untamed steed,"
That I almost had forgot,
Hobbyhorse just think or say?—
Don't know what to do to-day.

—*Madison Cawain, "Nothing To Do"*

In what other sport do you put on leather boots, stretch-fabric breeches, a shirt and tie, a wool jacket, a velvet-covered cap, and leather gloves, and then go out and exercise?

—*A. London Wolf, on horse-showing
in 90-degree summer weather*

"Bitzer," said Thomas Gradgrind. "Your definition of a horse."

"Quadruped. Graminivorous. Forty teeth, namely twenty-four grinders, four eye-teeth, and twelve incisive. Sheds coat in the spring; in marshy countries, sheds hoofs, too. Hoofs hard, but requiring to be shod with iron. Age known by marks in mouth."

"Now girl number twenty," said Mr. Gradgrind. "You know what a horse is."

—*Charles Dickens*, Hard Times

An out-of-towner accidently drove his car into a deep ditch on the side of a country road. Luckily a farmer happened by with his big old horse named Benny. Seeing the problem, the farmer said Benny could pull his car out. He hitched Benny to the car bumper and yelled, "Pull, Nellie, pull!" Benny didn't move. Then he yelled, "Come on, Ranger, pull!" Still, Benny didn't move.

The farmer then said, "Okay, Benny, pull." Benny pulled the car out of the ditch. The man was very appreciative but curious, and he asked why the farmer called his horse by the wrong name twice.

The farmer replied, "Benny doesn't see very well anymore, and if he thought he was the only one pulling he wouldn't even try."

—*Source unknown*

"You know, Doctor," said the horse, "that vet over the hill knows nothing at all. He has been treating me six weeks now—for spavins. What I need is spectacles. I am going blind in one eye. There's no reason why horses shouldn't wear glasses, the same as people.
                              —*Hugh Lofting*, Doctor Dolittle

A cowboy describing why he bailed off a bronco he was trying to break: "The first buck, he bucked so hard, I lost my stirrups. Then he bucked so high his left hind foot got into the left stirrup. Well, sir, I figured if he's gettin' on, I'm gettin' off."
                              —*Source unknown*

I ride horses because it's the only sport where I can exercise while sitting down.
                              —*Joan Hansen*

I have a horse—a ryghte good horse—
Ne doe Y envye those
Who scoure ye playne yn headye course
Tyll soddayne on theyre nose
They lyghte wyth unexpected force
Yt ys—a horse of clothes.

I have a saddel—"Say'st thou soe?
Wyth styrruppes, Knyghte, to boote?"
I sayde not that—I answere "Noe"—
Yt lacketh such, I woote:
Yt ys a mutton-saddel, loe!
Parte of ye fleecye brute.

I have a bytte—a ryghte good bytte—
As shall bee seene yn tyme.
Ye jawe of horse yt wyll not fytte;
Yts use ys more sublyme.
Fayre Syr, how deemest thou of yt?
Yt ys—thys bytte of rhyme.

—*Lewis Carroll, "Ye Carpette Knyghte"*

It takes a good deal of physical courage to ride a horse. This, however, I have. I get it at about forty cents a flask, and take it as required.
    —*Stephen Leacock*, *"Reflections on Riding,"* Literary Lapses

I'd horsewhip you . . . if I had a horse.
    —*Groucho Marx (as Professor Quincey Adams Wagstaff)*
in the movie Horsefeathers

A horse that can count to ten is a remarkable horse, not a remarkable mathematician.
    —*Samuel Johnson, quoted in* Life of Samuel Johnson,
by James Boswell

"You hear of the city feller who wanted to board his horse and he asked his friends what he ought to pay and they said, 'The price ranges from one dollar a month to fifty cents to two bits, but whatever you pay you're entitled to the manure.'"

So this city feller goes to the first farmer, and the farmer says, "One dollar," and the city feller said, "But I get the manure?" The farmer nods, and at the next place it's fifty cents, and the city feller says, "But I get the manure?" and the farmer nods.

At the third farm two-bits and the same story, so the city feller says "Maybe I can find a place that's real cheap," and he goes to a broken-down farm and the man says, "Ten cents a month," and the city feller says, "But I get the manure?" and the farmer says, "Son, at ten cents a month there ain't gonna be any manure."

—*James Michener*, Centennial

Every horse thinks its own pack heaviest.

—*Thomas Fuller*

Pat: He was an Anglo-Irishman.
Meg: In the blessed name of God, what's that?
Pat: A Protestant with a horse.

—*Brendan Behan*, The Hostage

They head the list
Of bad to bet on,
But I insist
They're worse to get on.

—*Richard Armour, "Horses"*

Horse sense is the thing a horse has, which keeps it from betting on people.

—*W. C. Fields*

Ain't you never heard what Peter done?
Run the quarter-mile in twenty-one
And he run it backwards in twenty flat;
Why, stranger, where have you been at?
What else could he do,
This Peter McCue?
He could gallop the range with tireless legs,
He could build a fire and scramble the eggs;
Though he never learned to subtract or divide,
He was mighty good when he multiplied.
        —*Anonymous, "Peter McCue" [celebrating the versatility*
of a nineteenth-century Quarter Horse]

A fly, sir, may sting a stately horse, and make him wince; but one is but an insect, and the other a horse still.
        —*Samuel Johnson, in* The Life of Samuel Johnson,
by James Boswell

I have the experience to be Governor. I know how to play craps. I know how to play poker. I know how to go in and out of the Baptist Church and ride horses.

—*Governor Earl Long*

He flung himself on his horse and rode off madly in all directions.
—*Stephen Leacock*, Guido the Gimlet of Ghent

The old mare watched the tractor work
A thing of rubber and steel,
Ready to follow the slightest wish
Of the man who held the wheel.
She said to herself as it passed by,
You gave me an awful jolt
But there's still one thing you cannot do,
You cannot raise a colt.

—*Source unknown*

Riding: The art of keeping a horse between you and the ground.

—*Source unknown*

The daughter who won't lift a finger in the house is the same child who cycles madly off in the pouring rain to spend all morning mucking out a stable.

—*Sarah Armstrong*

A horse is dangerous at both ends and uncomfortable in the middle.

—*Ian Fleming*

You can tell a gelding, you can ask a mare, but you must discuss it with a stallion.

—*Source unknown*

One day in heaven Saint Peter, Saint Paul and Saint John were standing around near the horse paddocks watching the horses frolic. "I am certainly bored," stated John. "Me too," Paul chimed as Peter stood and watched the horses. "I know!" Peter began. "Why don't we have a horse show?"

Paul and John thought that the idea was great except for one small detail. "Whom are we to compete against?" Paul asked. The trio pondered a moment when Peter realized the answer. "We will call up Satan and invite him to the horse show. I mean, we have all of the finest horses here in heaven, all of the world and national champions are here. His stable is ridden with the spoiled, difficult and mean horses. We are certain to win."

And so the trio called up Satan and invited him to their horse show. Satan laughed and asked why they would want to be humiliated like that, because he would certainly beat them. Peter, Paul and John did not understand. "What do you mean?" Peter asked. "We have all the national and world champion horses in our stable in heaven. How could you possibly beat us?

Satan laughed. "Have you forgotten so soon, gentlemen? I have all the judges!"

—*Source unknown*

The rider
Is fat
As that ( )
Or wider ( )
In torso
Of course
The horse
Is more so ( )

—*Wey Robinson, "Horse & Rider"*

Speak kindly to your little horse,
And soothe him when he wheezes,
Or he may turn his back on you,
And kick you where he pleases.

—*Source unknown*

The old grey horse, dreaming as he plodded along, of his quiet paddock, in a new raw situation such as this simply abandoned himself to his natural emotions. Rearing, plunging, backing steadily, in spite of all the Mole's efforts at his head, and all the Mole's lively language directed at his better feelings, he drove the cart backwards towards the deep ditch at the side of the road.

—*Kenneth Grahame,* The Wind in the Willows

I know two things about the horse,
And one of them is rather coarse.

—*Source unknown*

The steed bit his master;
How came this to pass?
He heard the good pastor
Cry, "All flesh is grass."

—*Anonymous, "On a Clergyman's Horse Biting Him"*

One man's wrong lead is another man's counter-canter.

—*S. D. Price*

Want to end up with a million bucks in the horse business? Start out with five million.

—*Source unknown*

A camel is a horse designed by a committee.

—*Attributed to British economist Alec Issigoris*

To confess that you are totally ignorant about the horse is social suicide: you will be despised by everybody, especially the horse.

—*W. C. Sellar*

How do you catch a loose horse?
Make a noise like a carrot.

—British cavalry joke

~

I prefer a bike to a horse. The brakes are more easily checked.

—Lambert Jeffries

~

Well, the hillbillies beat the dudes and took the polo championship of the world right out of the drawing room and into the bunkhouse. And she won't go East in years.

Poor old society. They got nothing exclusive left. The movie folks outmarried and outdivorced 'em, the common folks took their cocktails, "near" society took to bridge. Now polo has gone to the buckwheat belt.

—Will Rogers, in a 1933 syndicated newspaper column
after a team of Western polo players soundly defeated a
team of the best of the Eastern "Establishment" players

~

Men are generally more careful of the breeding of their horses and dogs than of their children.

>   —William Penn, "Some Fruits of Solitude, in Reflections
>   and Maxims relating to the Conduct of Human Life"

I love the horse from hoof to head.
From head to hoof and tail to mane.
I love the horse as I have said—
From head to hoof and back again.

>   —James Whitcomb Riley

The tribal wisdoms of the Dakota Indians, passed on from generation to generation, says that "when you discover that you are riding a dead horse, the best strategy is to dismount." However, in many companies as well as in the UN and NGO community a range of far more advanced strategies are often employed, such as:

1. Changing riders

2. Appointing a committee to study the horse

3. Arranging to visit other countries to see how others ride dead horses

4. Lowering the standards so that dead horses can be included

5. Reclassifying the dead horse as "living impaired"

6. Hiring outside contractors to ride the dead horse

7. Harnessing several dead horses together to increase the speed

8. Providing additional funding and/or training to increase the dead horse's performance

9. Doing a productivity study to see if lighter riders would improve the dead horse's performance

10. Declaring that as the dead horse does not have to be fed, it is less costly, carries lower overhead, and therefore contributes substantially more to the mission of the organization than do some other horses

11. Rewriting the expected performance requirements for all horses

—*Dakota Indian tribal wisdom on project management*

You can lead a horse to water, but if you can teach him to roll over and float on his back, then you got something.

—*Joe E. Lewis*

That hoss wasn't built to tread the earth,
He took natural to the air,
And every time he went aloft,
He tried to leave me there.

—*"Anonymous Tribute to an Unmanageable Horse"*

Murphy's Laws of Horses:

    ◌ No one ever notices how you ride until you fall off.

    ◌ The least useful horse in your barn will eat the most grain, require shoes every four weeks and need the vet at least once a month.

∽ A horse's misbehavior will be in direct proportion to the number of people who are watching.

∽ Clipper blades become dull just as your horse is half clipped.

∽ When wearing clean clothes, if you approach your barn within fifty feet, the clothes will be soiled.

∽ The number of horses you will own increases in direct proportion to the stalls in your barn.

∽ Baling twine keeps the world together.

∽ There is no such thing as a sterile barn cat.

∽ Hoof picks always run away from home.

∽ If you fall off, you will land on the site of your most recent injury.

Mark Twain was no great friend to horses, as the follow utterances demonstrate:

My experience of horses is that they never throw away a chance to go lame, and that in all respects they are well meaning and unreliable animals. I have also observed that if you refuse a high price for a favorite horse, he will go and lay down somewhere and die.

I know the horse too well. I have known the horse in war and in peace, and there is no place where a horse is comfortable. A horse thinks of too many things to do which you do not expect. He is apt to bite you in the leg when you think he is half asleep. The horse has too many caprices, and he is too much given to initiative. He invents too many new ideas. No, I don't want anything to do with a horse.

I am not an expert in horses and do not speak with assurance. I can always tell which is the front end of a horse, but beyond that my art is not above the ordinary.

If the horses knew their strength we should not ride anymore.
I am one of the poorest horsemen in the world, and I never mount a horse without experiencing a sort of dread that I may be setting out on that last mysterious journey which all of us must take sooner or later, and I never come back in safety from a horseback trip without thinking of my latter end for two or three days afterward.

III

LITERATURE
AND
POETRY

I on my horse, and Love on me, doth try
Our horsemanships, while by strange work I prove
A horseman to my horse, a horse to Love,
And now man's wrongs in me, poor beast! decry.
The reins wherewith my rider doth me tie
Are humbled thoughts, which bit of reverence move,
Curb'd-in with fear, but with gilt bosse above
Of hope, which makes it seem fair to the eye:
The wand is will; thou, Fancy, saddle art,
Girt fast by Memory; and while I spur
My horse, he spurs with sharp desire my heart.
He sits me fast however I do stir,
And now hath made me to his hand so right,
That in the manage myself take delight.

—*Sir Philip Sidney, sonnet #49,*
"Astrophel and Stella" sonnet cycle

Steeds, steeds, what steeds! Has the whirlwind a home in
your manes?

—*Nikolai Gogol,* Dead Souls

Their horses were of great stature, strong and clean-limbed; their grey coats glistened, their long tails flowed in the wind, their manes were braided on their proud necks.

—*J.R.R. Tolkien*, The Lord of the Rings,
The Two Towers

Round-hoof'd, short-jointed, fetlocks shag and long,
Broad breast, full eye, small head, and nostril wide,
High crest, short ears, straight legs and passing strong,
Thin mane, thick tail, broad buttock, tender hide:
Look, what a horse should have he did not lack,
Save a proud rider on so proud a back.

—*William Shakespeare*, Venus and Adonis, *lines 259–300*

What do we, as a nation, care about books? How much do you think
we spend altogether on our libraries, public or private, as compared
what we spend on our horses?

—*John Ruskin*, Sesame and Lilies

Some Moorish barb was that mustang's sire. His lines were beyond
  all wonder.
From the prick of his ears to the flow of his tail he ached in my
  throat and eyes.
Steel and velvet grace! As the prophet says, God had "clothed his
  neck with thunder."
Oh, marvelous with the drifting cloud he drifted across the skies!

—*Stephen Rose Benet*, "*The Horse Thief*"

In that expectation I walked my panting Lithuanian to a spring in this market-place, and let him drink. He drank uncommonly, with an eagerness not to be satisfied, but natural enough; for when I looked round for my men, what should I see, gentlemen! the hind part of the poor creature-croup and legs were missing, as if he had been cut in two, and the water ran out as it came in, without refreshing or doing him any good! How it could have happened was quite a mystery to me, till I returned with him to the town-gate. There I saw, that when I rushed in pell-mell with the flying enemy, they had dropped the portcullis (a heavy falling door, with sharp spikes at the bottom, let down suddenly to prevent the entrance of an enemy into a fortified town) unperceived by me, which had totally cut off his hind part, that still lay quivering on the outside of the gate. It [the separation of the Baron's horse's hindquarters from its forequarters] would have been an irreparable loss, had not our farrier contrived to bring both parts together while hot. He sewed them up with sprigs and young shoots of laurels that were at hand; the wound healed, and, what could not have happened but to so glorious a horse, the sprigs took root in his body, grew up, and formed a bower over me; so that afterwards I could go upon many other expeditions in the shade of my own and my horse's laurels.

—*Rudolph Raspe*, The Travels of Baron Munchhausen

We rode through endless thickets of yellow-pollened cassi—if riding it could be called; for those fragrant thickets were inhabited by wasps. And such wasps! Great yellow fellows the size of small canary birds, darting through the air with behind them drifting a bunch of legs a couple of inches long. A stallion abruptly stands on his forelegs and thrusts his hind legs skyward. He withdraws them from the sky long enough to make one wild jump ahead, and then returns them to their index position. It is nothing. His thick hide has merely been punctured by a flaming lance of wasp virility. Then a second and a third stallion, and all the stallions, begin to cavort on their forelegs over the precipitous landscape.

—*Jack London*, The Cruise of the Snark

Suppose . . . and suppose that a wild little Horse of Magic
Came cantering out of the sky,
With bridle of silver and into the saddle I mounted
To fly—and to fly.

—*Walter de la Mare*, "Suppose"

Who doesn't look upward when searching for a name? Looking
  upward, what is there but the sky to see? And seeing it, how can
  the name or the hope be earthbound? Was there a horse named
  Pegasus that flew? Was there a horse with wings?
Yes, once there was—once, long ago, there was. And now there
  is again.

—Beryl Markham, "Was There A Horse with Wings?"

So, fair and softly, John he cried,
  But John he cried in vain;
That trot became a gallop soon,
  In spite of curb and rein.

So stooping down, as needs he must
  Who cannot sit upright,
He grasp'd the mane with both his hands,
  And eke with all his might.

His horse, who never in that sort
  Had handled been before,
What thing upon his back had got
  Did wonder more and more.

—William Cowper, "The Diverting History of John Gilpin"

He sent the flint stones flying, but the pony kept his feet,
He cleared the fallen timber in his stride,
And the man from Snowy River never shifted in his seat—
It was grand to see that mountain horseman ride.
Through the stringy barks and saplings, on the rough and
    broken ground,
Down the hillside at a racing pace he went;
And he never drew the bridle till he landed safe and sound,
At the bottom of that terrible descent.
                    —*Andrew Barton "Banjo" Paterson,*
                        "The Man from Snowy River"

Now whether the tall horse, in the natural playfulness of his
disposition, was desirous of having a little innocent recreation
with Mr. Winkle, or whether it occurred to him that he could
perform the journey as much to his own satisfaction without a
rider as with one, are points upon which, of course, we can arrive
at no distinct conclusion.
                    —*Charles Dickens,* The Pickwick Papers

Though I am an old horse, and have seen and heard a great deal, I never yet could make out why men are so fond of this sport; they often hurt themselves, often spoil good horses, and tear up the fields, and all for a hare, or a fox, or a stag, that they could get more easily some other way; but we are only horses, and don't know.

—*Anna Sewell*, Black Beauty

And now, to make the turn, Messala began to draw in his left-hand steeds, an act which necessarily slackened their speed. His spirit was high; more than one altar was richer of his vows; the Roman genius was still president. On the three pillars only six hundred feet away were fame, increase of fortune, promotions, and a triumph, ineffably sweetened by hate, all in store for him! That moment Malluch, in the gallery, saw Ben-Hur lean forward over his Arabs, and give them the reins. Out flew the many-folded lash in his hand; over the backs of the startled steeds it writhed and hissed, and hissed and writhed again and again; and though it fell not, there were both sting and menace in its quick report; and as the man passed thus from quiet to resistless action, his face suffused, his eyes gleaming, along the reins he seemed to flash his will; and instantly not one, but the four as one, answered with a leap that landed them alongside the Roman's car. . . . Above the noises of the race there was but one voice, and that was Ben-Hur's. In the old Aramaic, as the sheik himself, he called to the Arabs—

"On, Atair! On, Rigel! What, Antares! dost thou linger now? Good horse—oho, Aldebaran! I hear them singing in the tents. I hear the children singing and the women-singing of the stars, of Atair, Antares, Rigel, Aldebaran, victory!—and the song will never end. Well done! Home to-morrow, under the black tent—home!—On, Antares! The tribe is waiting for us, and the master is waiting! 'Tis done! 'tis done! Ha, ha! We have overthrown the proud. The hand that smote us in the dust. Ours the glory! Ha, ha!—steady! The work is done—soho! Rest!"

There had never been anything of the kind more simple; seldom anything so instantaneous.

—*Lew Wallace*, Ben-Hur

Then I cast loose my buff coat, each halter let fall,
Shook off both my jack-boots, let go belt and all,
Stood up in the stirrup, leaned, patted his ear,
Called my Roland his pet name, my horse without peer;
   lapped my hands, laughed and sang, any noise bad or good,
   Til at length into Aix Roland galloped and stood.
   —*Robert Browning, "How They Brought the News from Ghent"*

and this parody:

I unsaddled the saddle, unbuckled the bit,
Unshackled the bridle (the bit didn't fit)
And ungalloped, ungalloped, ungalloped, ungalloped a bit.
          —*R. J. Yeatman and W. C. Sellar,*
          "How I Brought the Good News from
          Aix to Ghent (or Vice Versa)"

But he, mighty man, lay mightily in the whirl of dust, forgetful
of his horsemanship.

—*Homer*, The Iliad

A horse! A horse! My kingdom for a horse!
—*William Shakespeare*, Richard III, *Act V, Scene 4*

Spur not an unbroken horse.

—*Sir Walter Scott*, The Monastery

A small, select aristocracy, born booted and spurred to ride, and a
large dim mass born saddled and bridled to be ridden.

—*A.G. Gardiner*, Prophets, Priests and Kings
[the reference is to Great Britain before World War I]

Once more upon the water, yet once more!
And the waves bound beneath me as a steed
That knows his rider!

—*Lord Byron, "Childe Harold's Pilgrimage"*

There are a great many kinds of men; there are good, thoughtful
men, like our master, that any horse would be proud to serve; but
there are bad, cruel men, who never ought to have a horse or dog
to call their own. Besides, there are a great many foolish men, vain,
ignorant and careless, who never trouble themselves to think; these
spoil more horses than all, just for want of sense; they don't mean it,
but they do it for all that. I hope you will fall into good hands; but a
horse never knows who may buy him, or who may drive him; it is all
a chance for us, but still I say, do your best wherever it is, and keep
up your good name.

—*Anna Sewell,* Black Beauty

Gamaun is a dainty steed,
Strong, black, and of a noble breed,
Full of fire, and full of bone,
With all his line of fathers known;
Fine his nose, his nostrils thin,
But blown abroad by the pride within;
His mane is like a river flowing,
And his eyes like embers glowing
In the darkness of the night,
And his pace as swift as light.

*—Barry Cornwall (pseudonym of Bryan
Waller Procter)*, The Blood Horse

The sunshine's golden gleam is thrown
On sorrel, chestnut, bay and roan;
The horses prance and paw and neigh,
Fillies and colts like kittens play,
And dance and toss their rippled manes
Shining and soft as silken skeins.

*—Oliver Wendell Holmes, Sr.,
"How the Old Horse Won the Bet"*

Then came forward the Persian sage and, prostrating himself before the King, presented him with a horse of the blackest ebony-wood inlaid with gold and jewels, and ready harnessed with saddle, bridle and stirrups such as befit Kings; which when Sabur saw, he marvelled with exceeding marvel and was confounded at the beauty of its form and the ingenuity of its fashion. So he asked, "What is the use of this horse of wood, and what is its virtue and what the secret of its movement?"; and the Persian answered, "O my lord, the virtue of this horse is that, if one mount him, it will carry him whither he will and fare with its rider through the air and cover the space of a year in a single day."

—Arabian Nights, *"The Ebony Horse"*

And then it happened. It was like the release of a coiled watch-spring; the black whirled as a top spins and Strann sagged far to the left; before he could recover the stallion was away in a flash, like a racer leaving the barrier and reaching full speed in almost a stride. Not far—hardly the breadth of the street—before he pitched up in a long leap as if to clear a barrier, landed stiff-legged with a sickening jar, whirled again like a spinning top, and darted straight back. . . . When the stallion dropped stiff-legged, [Strann] was thrown forward and an unlucky left foot jarred loose from the stirrup; and when the horse whirled Strann was flung from the saddle. It was a clean fall. He twisted over in the air as he fell and landed in deep dust. The black stallion had reached his master and now he turned, in that same catlike manner, and watched with pricking ears as Strann dragged himself up from the dust.

—*Max Brand*, The Night Horseman

. . . She snapped a picture of Borina in the splash of sunlight at the full height of his courbette. Afterward she sent it to Hans, framed in red velvet. Underneath the picture she had written in her beautiful handwriting: "He bounds from the earth with the very exuberance of his spirits."

—*Xenophon*

Hans examined the picture carefully, slowly. He studied the angle of the leap, the position of the haunches, the hocks, the bend of the forelegs, the arch of the neck. Then he looked at the rider. The face did not show. It might have been himself, or anyone he knew, or no one. The rider had somehow extinguished himself in order to glorify the horse, to make him look as if he had performed of his own will— joyously, gaily.

Now, at last, Hans understood the mystery.

—*Marguerite Henry*, The White Stallions of Lipizza

The little bright mare, made of nerves and steel springs,
Shot level beside him, shot ahead as with wings.
Charles felt his horse quicken, felt the desperate beat
Of the blood in his body from his knees to his feet.

—*John Masefield*, *"Right Royal"*

The Scythian cavalry regiments indeed resound with famous stories
of horses: a chieftain was challenged to a duel by an enemy and
killed, and when his adversary came to strip his body of his armor,
his horse kicked him and bit him till he died; another horse, when his
blinkers were removed and it found out that the mare he had covered
was his dam, made for a precipice and committed suicide.

—*Pliny The Elder*, Natural History

The ego's relation to the id might be compared to that of the rider to his horse. The horse supplies the locomotive energy, while the rider has the privilege of deciding on the goal and of guiding the powerful animal's movement.

—*Sigmund Freud*, New Introductory
Lectures on Psycho-Analysis

As some swift horse
Is reined in by his rider, when he strains
Unto the race-course, and he neighs, and champs
The curbing bit, dashing his chest with foam,
And his feet eager for the course are still
Never, his restless hooves are clattering aye;
His mane is a stormy cloud, he tosses high
His head with snortings, and his lord is glad;

—*Quintus Smyrnaeus, "The Fall of Troy"*

Come off to the stable, all you who are able,
And give your horses some oats and some corn;
For if you don't do it, your colonel will know it,
And then you will rue it, as sure as you're born.

>   —*Words to the "Stable Call" cavalry bugle call*

Ay, they heard his foot upon the stirrup,
And the sound of iron on stone
And how the silence surged softly backward
When the plunging hoofs were gone.

>   —*Walter de la Mare, "The Listeners"*

Of coursers also spake they: Henry rid
Well, like most Englishmen, and loved the races;
And Juan, like a true-born Andalusian,
Could back a horse, as despots ride a Russian.

>   —*Lord Byron*, Don Juan, Canto 13

Horses live on dry land, eat grass and drink water. When pleased, they rub necks together. When angry, they turn round and kick up their heels at each other. Thus far only do their natural dispositions carry them. But bridled and bitted, with a plate of metal on their foreheads, they learn to cast vicious looks, to turn the head to bite, to resist, to get the bit out of the mouth or the bridle into it. And their natures become depraved.

—Chuang Tzu

But hollow men, like horses hot at hand,
Make gallent show and promise of their mettle;
But when they should endure the bloody spur,
They fall their crests, and like deceitful jades,
Sink in the trial.

—William Shakespeare, Julius Caesar, *Act IV, Scene* 2

She felt the eyes of that horse; great glowing, fearsome eyes,
arched with a question, and containing a white blade of light
like a threat. What was his non-human question, and his uncanny
threat? She didn't know. He was some splendid demon, and she
must worship him.

—*D. H. Lawrence*, St. Mawr

Whose laughs are hearty, tho' his jests are coarse,
And loves you best of all things—but his horse.

—*Alexander Pope, "Epistle to Miss Blount"*

If some beggar steals a bridle
he'll be hung by a man who's stolen a horse.
There's no surer justice in the world than that
which makes the rich thief hang the poor one.

—*Peire Cardenal (c. 1180–1272), French troubadour poet*

My horses understand me tolerably well; I converse with them at least four hours every day. They are strangers to bridle or saddle; they live in great amity with me, and friendship of each other.

—*Jonathan Swift,* Gulliver's Travels

I had a little pony,
His name was Dapple Gray;
I lent him to a lady
To ride a mile away;
She whipped him, she slashed him,
She rode him through the mire;
I would not lend my pony now
For all the lady's hire.

—*Anonymous, "I Had a Little Pony"*

Rise from the ground like feather'd Mercury,
And vaulted with such ease into his seat
As if an angel dropp'd down from the clouds,
And turn and wind a fiery Pegasus
And witch the world with noble horsemanship.
    —*William Shakespeare*, Henry IV, *Part One Act IV, Scene 1*

Hurrah, hurrah for Sheridan! Hurrah, hurrah for horse and man!
And when their statues are placed on high
Under the dome of the Union sky,
The American soldier's Temple of Fame,
There with the glorious General's name
Be it said in letters both bold and bright:
"Here is the steed that saved the day
By carrying Sheridan into the fight
From Winchester,—twenty miles away!"
        —*Thomas Buchanan Read, "Sheridan's Ride"*

The colt in the Long Meadow kicked up his heels.
"That was a fly," he thought. "it's early for flies."
But being alive, in April, was too fine
For flies or anything else to bother a colt.
He kicked up his heels again, this time in pure joy,
And started to run a race with the wind and his shadow.
                    —*Stephen Vincent Benet, "John Brown's Body"*

Oh, a wonderful horse is the Fly-Away Horse—
Perhaps you have seen him before;
Perhaps, while you slept, his shadow has swept
Through the moonlight that floats on the floor.
For it's only at night, when the stars twinkle bright,
That the Fly-Away Horse, with a neigh
And a pull at his rein and a toss of his mane,
Is up on his heels and away!
                    —*Eugene Field, "The Fly-Away Horse"*

So hurry to see your lady,
Like a stallion on the track

—*Love song of the New Kingdom of ancient Egypt*

Now the world is white, go it while you're young,
Take the girls tonight, and sing this sleighing song:
Just get a bob-tailed nag, two-forty for his speed,
Then hitch him to an open sleigh, and crack! You'll take the lead.

—*J. Pierpont, "Jingle Bells" ["two-forty"*
refers to the time the horse would trot a mile]

The mare soon after my entrance rose from her mat, and coming
up close, after having nicely observed my hands and face, gave
me the most contemptuous look, and turning to the horse, I heard
the word Yahoo often repeated twixt them; the meaning of which
I could not comprehend. . . .

—*Jonathan Swift,* Gulliver's Travels

A man in passion rides a mad horse.
　　　　　—*Benjamin Franklin*, Poor Richard's Almanack

In Aberdeenshire the last sheaf [of wheat] or "Maiden" is carried
home in merry procession by the harvesters. It is then presented to
the mistress of the house, who dresses it up to be preserved until the
first mare foals. The Maiden is then taken down and presented to
the mare as its first food. The neglect of this would have untoward
effects upon the foal. . . .
　　　　　—*Sir James Frazer*, The Golden Bough

Today, all day, I rode upon the down,
With hounds and horsemen, a brave company
On this side in its glory lay the sea,
On that the Sussex weald, a sea of brown.
The wind was light, and brightly the sun shone,
And still we gallop'd on from gorse to gorse:
And once, when check'd, a thrush sang, and my horse
Prick'd his quick ears as to a sound unknown.
I knew the Spring was come. I knew it even
Better than all by this, that through my chase
In bush and stone and hill and sea and heaven
I seem'd to see and follow still your face.
Your face my quarry was. For it I rode,
My horse a thing of wings, myself a god.

—*Wilfrid Blunt,* "*St. Valentine's Day*"

But the worst of all is that when his harness is once on, he may
neither jump for joy nor lie down for weariness. So you see this
breaking in is a great business.

—*Anna Sewell,* Black Beauty

Yet, if you enter the woods
Of a summer evening late,
When the night-air cools on the trout-ringed pools
Where the otter whistles his mate.
They fear not men in the woods,
Because they see so few
You will hear the beat of a horse's feet,
And the swish of a skirt in the dew,
Steadily cantering through
The misty solitudes,
As though they perfectly knew
The old lost road through the woods. . . .

    —*Rudyard Kipling, "The Road Through the Woods"*

Who shall declare the joy of the running!
Who shall tell of the pleasures of flight!
Springing and spurning the tufts of wild heather,
Sweeping, wide-winged, through the blue dome of light.
Everything mortal has moments immortal,
Swift and God-gifted, immeasurably bright.

So with the stretch of the white road before me,
Shining snowcrystals rainbowed by the sun,
Fields that are white, stained with long, cool, blue shadows,
Strong with the strength of my horse as we run.
Joy in the touch of the wind and the sunlight!
Joy! With the vigorous earth I am one.

—*Amy Lowell, "A Winter Ride"*

The animal [Ichabod Crane] bestrode was a broken-down plough-horse, that had outlived almost every thing but his viciousness. He was gaunt and shagged, with a ewe neck and a head like a hammer; his rusty mane and tail were tangled and knotted with burrs; one eye had lost its pupil, and was glaring and spectral; but the other had the gleam of a genuine devil in it. Still he must have had fire and mettle in his day, if we may judge from the name he bore of Gunpowder. He had, in fact, been a favorite steed of his master's, the choleric Van Ripper, who was a furious rider, and had infused, very probably, some of his own spirit into the animal; for, old and broken-down as he looked, there was more of the lurking devil in him than in any young filly in the country.

—*Washington Irving*, The Legend of Sleepy Hollow

I had a gig-horse, and I called him Pleasure
Because on Sundays for a little jaunt
He was so fast and showy, quite a treasure;
Although he sometimes kicked and shied aslant.
I had a chaise, and christened it Enjoyment,
With yellow body and the wheels of red,
Because it was only used for one employment,
Namely, to go wherever Pleasure led.

—*Thomas Hood*, "Allegory"

We've had a stirring life, old woman!
You, and I, and the old grey horse.
Races, and fairs, and royal occasions. . . .

—*George Meredith*, "Juggling Jerry"

Take care to sell your horse before he dies. The art of life is passing
losses on.

—*Robert Frost*, The Ingenuities of Debt

Must we drag on this stupid existence forever,
So idly and weary, so full of remorse,
While everyone else takes his pleasure, and never
Seems happy unless he is riding a horse?

      —*Edward Lear,* Laughable Lyrics

"Will you lend me your mare to go a mile?"
"No, she is lame leaping over a stile."
"But if you will her to me spare,
You should have money for your mare."
"Oh ho, say you so?
Money will make the mare go."

       —*Old English song*

I wheeled about,
Proud and exulting like an untired horse
That cares not for his home.

   —*William Wordsworth, "Influence of Natural Objects*
    in Calling Forth and Strengthening the Imagination
     in Boyhood and Early Youth"

He will hold thee, when his passion shall have spent its novel force,
Something better than his dog, a little dearer than his horse.

—*Alfred Tennyson*, Locksley Hall

I will not change my horse with any that treads on four pasterns. Ca,
ha! He bounds from the earth, as if his entrails were hairs, le cheval
volant, the Pegasus, chez les narines de feu! When I bestride him, I
soar, I am a hawk: he trots the air; the earth sings when he touches it;
the basest horn of his hoof is more musical than the pipe of Hermes
. . . he is pure air and fire...the prince of palfreys; his neigh is like the
bidding of a monarch and his countenance enforces homage.

—*William Shakespeare*, Henry V, Act III, Scene 7

The Colonel's son has taken a horse, and a raw rough dun was he,
With the mouth of a bell and the heart of Hell and the head of a
gallows-tree.

—*Rudyard Kipling*, The Ballad of East and West

And, even when she turn'd, the curse
Had fallen, and her future Lord
Was drown'd in passing thro' the ford,
Or kill'd in falling from his horse.

—Alfred, Lord Tennyson, "In Memorium: A.A.H."

For, look you, my horse is good to prance
A right fair measure in this war-dance,
Before the eyes of Philip of France;
Ah! qu'elle est belle La Marguerite.

—William Morris, "The Eve of Crecy"

That is Shadowfax. He is chief of the Maeras, lords of all horses, and not even Theoden, King of Rohan, has ever looked on a better. Does he not shine like silver, and run as smoothly as a swift stream?

—J. R. R. Tolkien

The Associated Press reports carrying the news of Mary White's death declared that it came as a result from the fall from a horse. How she would have hooted at that! She never fell from a horse in her life. Horses have fallen on her and with her—"I'm always trying to hold 'em in my lap," she used to say. But she was proud of few things, and one was that she could ride anything that had four legs and hair.

—William Allen White, "Mary White"
[the newspaper editor's obituary for his daughter]

Such horses are
The jewels of the horseman's hands and thighs,
They go by the word and hardly need the rein.
They bred such horses in Virginia then,
Horses that were remembered after death
And buried not so far from Christian ground
That if their sleeping riders should arise
They could not witch them from the earth again
And ride a printless course along the grass
With the old manage and light ease of hand.

—Stephen Vincent Benet, "John Brown's Body"

Mr. Lamb thought of his best pyjamas, and throwing back his head gave vent to a wild neigh. He was feeling rather wild, and at the same time a trifle timid. He had often played horses as a child, but never actually been one . . .

He rose from his strange position and backed away from the mirror, but was still unable to get the desired view. Bending an eloquent glance upon his daughter, he pointed with his hoof to the mirror. Obediently the girl went over to the mirror, and after much shaking and nodding of her father's head, she adjusted it to his satisfaction.

"That's something like," thought Lamb, surveying his reflection with no little satisfaction.

He was a fine body of a horse—a sleek, strapping stallion. Black as night with a star on his forehead. He turned slowly, taking himself in from all angles.

"Rather indecent, though," he thought. "Wish I had a blanket, a long one. Oh, Hell! I'm a horse, now. Horses don't mind. Still it doesn't seem quite—well, I just never did it before, that's all." He paused to reconsider his reflection, then continued his soliloquy. "Anyway, if that girl can go about in step-ins and such, I can go about in nothing at all."

— *Thorne Smith*, The Stray Lamb

Sometimes, if the work horses were to be used that day, Jody
found Billy Buck in the barn harnessing and currying. Billy stood
with him and looked long at Gabilan and he told Jody a great many
things about horses . . . He told Jody how horses love conversation.
He must talk to the pony all the time, and tell him the reasons for
everything. Billy wasn't sure that a horse could understand everything
that was said to him, but irt was impossible to say how much was
understood. A horse never kicked up a fuss if someone he liked
explained things to him.

—*John Steinbeck*, The Red Pony

But, after the war was over, just think what came to pass—
A letter, sir; and the two were safe back in the old Bluegrass.
The lad had got across the border, riding Kentucky Belle;
And Kentuck she was thriving, and fat, and hearty, and well;
He cared for her, and kept her, nor touched her with whip or spur;
Ah! we've had many horses, but never a horse like her!

—*Constance Fenimore Woolson*, Kentucky Belle

Those that tame wild horses
Pace 'em not in their hands to make 'em gentle,
But strip their mouths with stubborn bits, and spur 'em
Till they obey the menage.
　　　　—William Shakespeare, King Henry VIII, *Act V, Scene 3*

Cast a cold eye
On life, on death.
Horseman, pass by!

　　　　　　　—William Butler Yeats "Under Ben Bulben"
　　　　　　　[these lines are inscribed on Yeats's headstone]

The revolution does not choose its paths: it made its first steps
toward victory under the belly of a Cossack's horse.
　　　　—Leon Trotsky, History of the Russian Revolution

A short life in the saddle, Lord!
Not long life by the fire.
—*Louise Imogen Guiney, "The Knight Errant"*

I smell her still, I see her still, I hear the way she used to move about at night. What horse is ever so old as to forget his dam?
—*John Hawkes*, Sweet William

In his day he had been a star on the Georgia Tech football team. Football had left him with a banged-up right knee, that had turned arthritic about three years ago. . . . One of the beauties of the Tennessee walking horse was that its gait spared you from having to post, to pump up and down at the knees when the horse trotted. He wasn't sure he could take posting on this chilly February morning.
—*Tom Wolfe*, A Man in Full

There where the course is,
Delight makes all of the one mind,
The riders upon the galloping horses,
The crowd that closes in behind. . . .

> —*William Butler Yeats, "At Galway Races"*

Those lumbering horses in the steady plough,
On the bare field—I wonder why, just now,
They seemed terrible, so wild and strange,
Like magic power on the stony grange.

> —*Edwin Muir*, Horses

I jest to Oberon, and make him smile
When I a fat and bean-fed horse beguile,
Neighing in likeness of a filly foal.

> —*William Shakespeare*, A Midsummer
> Night's Dream, *Act II, Scene 1*

Nothing made the horse so fat as the king's eye.

—*Plutarch*, Life of Cicero

Yet if man, of all the Creator plann'd
His noblest work is reckoned,
Of the works of His hand, by sea or land,
The horse may at least rank second.

—*Adam Lindsay Gordon*, *"Hippondromania"*

At one time the Horse had the plain entirely to himself. Then a Stag intruded into his domain and shared his pasture. The Horse, desiring to revenge himself on the stranger, asked a man if he were willing to help him in punishing the Stag. The man replied that if the Horse would receive a bit in his mouth and agree to carry him, he would contrive effective weapons against the Stag.

The Horse consented and allowed the man to mount him. From that hour he found that instead of obtaining revenge on the Stag, he had enslaved himself to the service of man.

—*Aesop's Fables*, *"The Horse and the Stag"*

Then hey for boot and horse, lad,
And round the world away!
Young blood must have its course, lad,
And every dog his day.

—*Charles Kingsley, "Young And Old"*

Young hot colts being raged do rage the more.
—*William Shakespeare,* King Richard II, *Act II, Scene 1*

Dosnt thou 'ear my 'erse's legs, as they canters away?
Proputty, proputty, proputty—that's what I 'ears 'em say.
Proputty, proputty, proputty—Sam, thou's an ass for thy pains:
Theer's moor sense i' one o' 'is legs, nor in all thy brains.

—*Alfred, Lord Tennyson, "Northern Farmer: New Style"*

Things are in the saddle,
And ride mankind.
—*Ralph Waldo Emerson*, *"Ode (inscribed to W. H. Channing)"*

Well, it seemed to me stealing a horse for a ride was not the same thing as stealing something else, such as money. For all I knew, maybe it wasn't stealing at all. If you were crazy about horses the way my cousin Mourad and I were, it wasn't stealing. It wouldn't be stealing until we offered to sell the horse, which of course I knew we would never do.
—*William Saroyan*, The Summer of
the Beautiful White Horse

"What need I got for a horse I would need a bear trap to catch?" Eck said.
"Didn't you just see me catch him?"
"I seen you," Eck said. "And I don't want nothing as big as a horse if I got to wrastle with it every time it finds me on the same side of the fence it's on."
—*William Faulkner*, *"Spotted Horses"*

To battle rode George Washington
Upon my grandsire's courser,
And when the victory was won
The courser was no more, sir.

That faithful steed had borne our race
In saddle, chaise and pillion;
My father never saw his face,
But called him worth a million.

—*J. W. DeForest, "Judge Boodle"*

I wish your horses swift and sure of foot;
And so I do command you to their backs.

—*William Shakespeare*, Macbeth, *Act III, Scene 1*

But when the pony moved his legs,
Oh! then for the poor idiot boy!
For joy he cannot hold the bridle,
For joy his head and heels are idle,
He's idle all for very joy.

And while the pony moves his legs,
In Johnny's left-hand you may see,
The green bough's motionless and dead;
The moon that shines above his head
Is not more still and mute than he.

His heart it was so full of glee,
That till full fifty yards were gone,
He quite forgot his holly whip,
And all his skill in horsemanship,
Oh! happy, happy, happy John.

—*William Wordsworth and Samuel Taylor Coleridge,*
Lyrical Ballads, "The Idiot Boy"

Show me a man who has no pity on his horse, and I will show you one who is a cruel husband, if he is married, and a tyrannical parent, if he has children; a man that would be Nero if he had the power. He is a coward by nature and a fiend by practice.

—*George Eliot*, Middlemarch

The love of horses which they had, alive,
And care of chariots, after death survive.

—*Virgil*, The Aeneid

Ay, the horses trample,
The harness jingles now;
No change though you lie under
The land you used to plough.

—*A. E. Housman, "A Shropshire Lad"*

. . . but at Apollo's pleading
If that my Pegasus should not be founder'd,
I think to canter gently through a hundred.

—*Lord Byron*, Don Juan, Canto Twelve

You could see the warm, moist breath—the radiant and peaceful breath that came from the tremulous, life-filled, flaring nostrils of stallions and mares in the cold of certain dawns.

—*Clarice Lispector, "Dry Point of Horses"*

My cousin Mourad was sitting on a beautiful white horse.

I stuck my head out of the window and rubbed my eyes.

Yes, he said in Armenian. It's a horse. You're not dreaming. Make it quick if you want to ride.

I knew my cousin Mourad enjoyed being alive more than anybody else who had ever fallen into the world by mistake, but this was more than even I could believe.

In the first place, my earliest memories had been memories of horses and my first longings had been longings to ride. This was the wonderful part.

In the second place, we were poor.

—*William Saroyan*, The Summer of
the Beautiful White Horse

Like unback'd colts, they prick'd their ears,
Advanced their eryelids, lifted up their noses
As they smelled music.

—*William Shakespeare*, The Tempest, *Act IV, Scene 1*

Cicero said loud-bawling orators were driven by their weakness to noise, as lame men to take horse.

—*Plutarch*, Life of Cicero

Well could he ride, and often men would say
"That horse his mettle from his rider takes:
Proud of subjection, noble by the sway,
What rounds, what bounds, what course, what stop he makes!"
And controversy hence a question takes,
Whether the horse by him became his deed,
Or he his manage by the well-doing steed.

    —*William Shakespeare*, "A Lover's Complaint," lines 106–112

O the horseman's and horsewoman's joys!
The saddle, the gallop, the pressure upon the seat, the cool gurgling by the ears and hair.

—*Walt Whitman*, Leaves of Grass

Or on Pegasus mounted, well spurred and well booted,
With martingale fanciful, crupper poetic,
Saddle cloth airy, and whip energetic,
Girths woven of rainbows, and hard-twisted flax,
And horse-shoes as bright as the edge of an axe;
How blithe should she amble and prance on the road,
With a pillion behind . . .

> —*John Brainard, Written for a Lady's Commonplace-Book*

Agesilaus was very fond of his children; and it is reported that once toying with them he got astride upon a reed as upon a horse, and rode about the room; and being seen by one of his friends, he desired him not to speak of it till he had children of his own.

—*Plutarch*, Laconic Apophthegms of Agesilaus the Great

He doth nothing but talk of his horse.

> —*William Shakespeare*, The Merchant
> of Venice, *Act 1, Scene 2*

Some men to carriages aspire;
On some the costly hansoms wait;
Some seek a fly, on job or hire;
Some mount the trotting steed, elate.

—*Amy Levy, "Ballade of an Omnibus"*

Poor little foal of an oppressed race!
I love the languid patience of thy face.

—*Samuel Taylor Coleridge, "To a Young Ass"*

And next day I was able to lead my gray horse across the meadow to the spring, with my hand on his mane as my only guide—this "untamable outlaw" responded to my light touch. It was the simple truth—his mouth was too tender for a bridle bit. The pain just drove him wild; that's all that had made him an outlaw. Gentle handling, no loud shouts, no jerks on his tender mouth, good food and a cleaned skin—these spelled health and contentment. Kindness had conquered.

—Manuel Buaken, "The Horse of the Sword"

And when he spoke, he felt an affection for the little horse, an exultant pride in his courage, so different in quality from anything he had known before that it could not be described. It was more than sympathy, more than the bantering love of a friend; it was a feeling so strong that it seemed to have its own life, full of delight and worship; laughing at Satan and rejoicing in all devotion and courage; the mysterious greatness of the spirit.

—Joyce Cary, Bush River

Together, the two men start to edge the stallion forward. Tall as they are, they move like midgets beside his massive shoulders. He is the biggest thoroughbred that I have ever seen. He is the most beautiful. His coat is chestnut, flecked with white, and his mane and his tail are close to gold. There is a blaze on his face—wide and straight and forthright, as if by this marking he proclaims that he is none other than Rigel, for all his sins, for all the hush that begins to fall over the crowd.

He is Rigel and he looks upon the men who hold his chains as a captured king may look upon his captors. He is not tamed. Nothing about him promises that he will be tamed. Stiffly on reluctant hoofs, he enters the ring and flares his crimson nostrils at the crowd, and the crowd is still. The crowd whose pleasure is the docile beast of pretty paddocks, the gainly horse of cherished prints that hang upon the best hung walls, the willing winner of the race—upon the rebel this crowd stares, and the rebel stares it back.

—*Beryl Markham, "The Splendid Outcast"*

Let the galled jade wince, our withers are unrung.
    —*William Shakespeare*, Hamlet, *Act III, Scene* 2

The youth walks up to the white horse, to put its halter on and
the horse looks at him in silence. They are so silent, they are in
another world.

    —*D.H. Lawrence*, The White Horse

A monk there was, one made for mastery,
An outrider, who loved his venery;
A manly man, to be an abbot able.
Full many a blooded horse had he in stable:
And when he rode men might his bridle hear
A-jingling in the whistling wind as clear,
Aye, and as loud as does the chapel bell.
    —*Geoffrey Chaucer, Prologue to* The Canterbury Tales

And there lay the steed with his nostril all wide,
But through it there rolled not the breath of his pride;
And the foam of his gasping lay white on the turf,
And cold as the spray of the rock-beating surf.
—*George Gordon Noel, Lord Byron,*
"The Destruction of Sennacherib"

The Vizier proud, distinguish'd o'er the rest!
Six slaves in gay Attire his Bridle hold;
His Bridle rough with Gems, his Stirrups Gold;
His Snowy Steed adorn'd with lavish Pride
Whole Troops of Soldiers mounted by his Side,
These toss the Plumy Crest, Arabian Coursers guide.
—*Lady Mary Wortley Montague, "Constantinople"*

My little horse must think it queer
To stop without a farmhouse near
Between the woods and frozen lake
The darkest evening of the year.
    —*Robert Frost, "Stopping by Woods on a Snowy Evening"*

Her chariot is an empty hazel-nut
Made by the joiner squirrel or old grub,
Time out of mind the fairies' coachmakers.
And in this state she gallops night by night
Through lovers' brains, and then they dream of love.
    —*William Shakespeare*, Romeo and Juliet, *Act I, Scene 4*

The horses of Achilles stood apart from their battle weeping, because they had learned that their charioteer had fallen in the dust by the hand of man-slaying Hector. . . . When Zeus saw how they grieved, he took pity on them. "Poor creatures, why did I give you to King Peleus, a mortal destined to die—you who are immortal."
    —*Homer*, The Iliad

I give you horses for your games in May
And all of them well trained unto the course,
Each docile, swift, erect, a goodly horse;
With armour on their chests, and bells at play
Between their brows, and pennons fair and gay
Fine nets, and housings meet for warriors
Emblazoned with the shields ye claim for yours,
Gules, argent, or, all dizzy at noon day.

—*Attributed to Folgore di San Gimignano*

Since then 'tis centuries; but each
Feels shorter than the day
I first surmised the horses' heads
Were toward eternity.

—*Emily Dickinson, "The Chariot
("Because I Could Not Stop For Death)"*

He grew unto his seat; And to such wonderous doing brought
  his horse,
As he had been incorpsed and demi-natured
With the brave beast.
                    — *William Shakespeare*, Hamlet, *Act IV, Scene 7*

YOUTH, the circus-rider, fares gaily round the ring, standing
with one foot on the bare-backed horse—the Ideal. Presently, at
the moment of manhood, Life (exacting ring-master) causes another
horse to be brought in who passes under the rider's legs, and ambles
on. This is the Real. The young man takes up the reins, places a foot
on each animal, and the business now becomes serious.
                    —*Sidney Lanier, "Ambling, Ambling Round the Ring"*

With flowing tail and flying mane,
Wide nostrils, never stretched by pain,
Mouth bloodless to bit or rein,
And feet that iron never shod,
And flanks unscar'd by spur or rod.
A thousand horses—the wild—the free—
Like waves that follow o'er the sea,
Came thickly thundering on.
                    —*Lord Byron, "Child Harold's Pilgrimage"*

A horse misus'd upon the road
Calls to Heaven for human blood.
                    —*William Blake, "Auguries of Innocence"*

The smallest horse was the favorite, and when he saw her he
lifted his trim hind legs and shot them at the sides of the stall.
His delicate hooves ran like a regiment over the blackened timber.
He kicked in a frenzy, but his eyes were precisely on every move
she was making, and his teeth, small and sweet and unlike a horse's
teeth, were ready to smile. Even with his ears flat as a rabbit's as
he kicked, there was a flicker of knowledge in the tips of them that
waited patiently for her decision of whether she would fling the
saddle over him or whether she would go on to another stall,
leacing him ready to cry with impatience.

—*Kay Boyle, "Episode in the Life of an Ancestor"*

The kites of olden times, as well as the swans, had the privilege
of song. But having heard the neigh of the horse, they were so
enchanted with the sound, that they tried to imitate it; and, in trying
to neigh, they forgot how to sing.

Moral: The desire for imaginary benefits often involves the loss of
present blessings.

—Aesop's Fables, *"The Kites and the Swans"*

Gallop apace, you fiery-footed steeds,
Toward Phoebus' lodging.

—*William Shakespeare*, Romeo and Juliet, *Act III, Scene 2*

Are you—poor, sick old ere your time—
Nearer one whit your own sublime
Than we who have never turned a rhyme?
Sing, riding's a joy!
For me, I ride

—*Robert Browning, "The Last Ride Together"*

One may lead a horse to water,
Twenty cannot make him drink.

—*Christina Rossetti, "Goblin Market"*

Somewhere, somewhere . . . in time's own space,
there must be some sweet, pastured place . . .
where creeks sing on . . . and tall trees grow,
Some paradise where horses go.
For by the love that guides my pen,
I know great horses live again.
> —*Stanley Harrison, "Gentlemen—The Horse!"*

The horses, mares, and frisking fillies,
Clad, all, in linen white as lilies.
> —*Robert Herrick, "The Hock Cart, or Harvest Home"*

And neigh like Boanerges;
Then, punctual as a star,
Stop—docile and omnipotent—
At its own stable door.

                —*Emily Dickinson, "The Railway Train"*

She rode Comanche badly, sitting him with no sense of ease or mastership, she let him jog this way or that as he wanted, and when he turned his captious neck homeward, because if he couldn't keep up with the others he would rather get back and brood by himself in the corral, she let him have his head for several yards before she could succeed in guiding him back to the narrow, sandy path that edged the lake. He despised her anyway because of the way her citified old-maid bottom bounced up and down on his back, sliding her weight first to this side, then to that, of the saddle.

                —*Tess Slesinger, "Relax Is All"*

As I ride, as I ride
Ne'er has spur my swift horse plied,
Yet his hide, streaked and pied,
As I ride, as I ride,
Shows where sweat has sprung and dried,
—Zebra-footed, ostrich-thighed—
How has vied stride with stride
As I ride, as I ride!
    —*Robert Browning, "Through the Metidja to Abd-el-Kadr"*

Mother dear, we cannot stay!
The wild white horses foam and fret.
        —*Matthew Arnold, "The Forsaken Merman"*

Horses and men are just alike.
There was my stallion, Billy Lee,
Black as a cat and trim as a deer,
With an eye of fire, keen to start,
And he could hit the fastest speed
Of any racer around Spoon River.
            —*Edgar Lee Master,* Spoon River Anthology

For of this savage race unbent
The ocean is the element.
Of old escaped from Neptune's car, full sure
Still with the white foam flick'd are they
And when the seas puff black from gray,
And ships part cables, loudly neigh
The stallions of the Camargue, all joyful in the roar.
　　　　　　—*George Meredith, "The Mares of the Camargue"*

Their [the Tartars'] horses are so well broken-in to quick changes
of movement, that upon the signal given, they instantly turn in
every direction; and by these rapid manoeuvers many victories have
been won.

　　　　　　—*Marco Polo*, The Diversities and
　　　　　　　　　　Marvels of the World

Boot, saddle, to horse and away!
Rescue my castle before the hot day
Brightens to blue from its silvery gray,
(Chorus)
Boot, saddle, to horse, and away!
—*Robert Browning, "Cavalier Tunes: Boot And Saddle"*

Hast thou given the horse strength? hast thou clothed his neck
    with thunder?
Canst thou make him afraid as a grasshopper? the glory of his
    nostrils is terrible.
He paweth in the valley, and rejoiceth in his strength: he goeth
    on to meet the armed men.
He mocketh at fear, and is not affrighted, neither turneth he back
    from the sword.
—*The Bible: Job 39: 9–22*

Beggers mounted run their horses to death.
—*William Shakespeare*, Henry VI, *Part Three Act I, Scene 4*
[similar to "Set a beggar on horseback and he will ride a gallop,"
Robert Burton, Anatomy of Melancholy, *and the German*
proverb, "Set a beggar on horseback, and he'll outride the Devil."]

Sidney often wondered if horses were even meant to be ridden at all.
It was always such a struggle.
The thing about the broncs, he realized—and he never realized
it until they were rolling on top of him in the dust, or rubbing him
off against a tree, or against the side of a barn, trying to break his
leg was that if the horses didn't get broke, tamed, they'd get wilder.
There was nothing as wild as a horse that had never been broken. It
just got meaner each day.

—*Rick Bass, "Wild Horses"*

Dear to me is my bonnie white steed;
Oft has he helped me at pinch of need.

—*Sir Walter Scott, "Rokeby"*

When walkin' down a city street,
　　Two thousand miles from home,
The pavestone hurtin' of the feet
　　That never ought to roam,
A pony just reached to one side
　　And grabbed me by the clothes;
He smelled the sagebrush, durn his hide!
　　You bet a pony knows!
　　　　　　　　—Arthur Chapman, "The Meeting"

Let the Sultan bring his famous horses,
　　Prancing with their diamond-studded reins;
They, my darling, shall not match thy fleetness
　　When they course with thee the desert-plains.
　　　　　　　　—Bayard Taylor, "Hassan to His Mare"

. . . the mare . . . then set off for home with the speed of a swallow, and going as smoothly and silently. I never had dreamed of such delicate motion, fluent, and graceful, and ambient, soft as the breeze flitting over the flowers but swift as the summer lightning.

—*R. D. Blackmore*, Lorna Doone

I think I learned this [not necessarily to follow the majority opinion] when, as a boy on horseback, my interest was not in the campus; it was beyond it; and I was dependent upon. Not the majority of boys, but myself and the small minority group that happened to have horses.

—*Lincoln Steffans*, The Autobiography of Lincoln Steffans

Fast rode the knight
With spurs, hot and reeking,
Ever waving an eager sword,
"To save my lady!"
Fast rode the knight,
And leaped from saddle to war.

—*Stephen Crane, "Fast Rode the Knight"*

Ichabod was a suitable figure for such a steed. He rode with short stirrups, which brought his knees nearly up to the pommel of the saddle; his sharp elbows stuck out like grasshoppers'; he carried his whip perpendicularly in his hand, like a sceptre, and, as his horse jogged on, the motion of his arms was not unlike the flapping of a pair of wings. A small wool hat rested on the top of his nose, for so his scanty strip of forehead might be called; and the skirts of his black coat fluttered out almost to the horse's tail. Such was the appearance of Ichabod and his steed, as they shambled out of the gate of Hans Van Ripper, and it was altogether such an apparition as is seldom to be met with in broad daylight.

—*Washington Irving,* The Legend of Sleepy Hollow

The roan horse is young and will learn: the roan horse buckles into harness and feels the foam on the collar at the end of a haul: the roan horse points four legs to the sky and rolls in the red clover. . . .

—*Carl Sandburg, "Potato Blossom Songs and Jigs"*

What a creature he was! Never have I felt such a horse between my knees. His great haunches gathered under him with every stride, and he shot forward ever faster and faster, stretched like a greyhound, while the wind beat in my face and whistled past my ears.
—*Sir Arthur Conan Doyle, "The Adventures of Brigadier Girard"*

A little colt-broncho, loaned to the farm
To be broken in time without fury or harm,
Yet black crows flew past you, shouting alarm,
Calling "beware" with lugubrious singing. . . .
—*Vachel Lindsay, "The Broncho That Would Not Be Broken"*

Time travels in divers paces with divers persons. I'll tell you who Time ambles withal, who Time trots withal, who Time gallops withal, and who he stands still withal.
—*William Shakespeare, As You Like It, Act III, Scene 2*

With flowing tail and flying mane,
Wide nostrils never stretch'd by pain,
Mouths bloodless to the bit or rein,
And feet that iron never shod,
And flanks unscarr'd by spur or rod,
A thousand horse, the wild, the free,
Like waves that follow o'er the sea,
Came thickly thundering on . . .
They stop, they start, they snuff the air,
Gallop a moment here and there,
Approach, retire, wheel round and round . . .

—Lord Byron, "Mazeppa"

Behold! in glittering show,
A gorgeous car of state!
The white-plumed steeds, in cloth of gold,
Bow down beneath its weight;
And the noble war-horse, led
Caparison'd along,
Seems fiercely for his lord to ask,
As his red eye scans the throng.

—Lydia Huntley Sigourney, "The Return
of Napoleon from St. Helena"

Go anywhere in England, where there are natural, wholesome, contented and really nice English people, and what do you always find? That the stables are the real centre of the household.
—*George Bernard Shaw*, Heartbreak House

While his rider every hand survey'd,
Sprung loose, and flew into an escapade;
Not moving forward, yet with every bound
Pressing, and seeming still to quit his ground.
—*John Dryden, "Absalom and Achitophel"*

I have seen the general dare the combers come closer
And make to ride his bronze horse out into the hoofs
and guns of the storm.

—*Carl Sandburg, "Bronzes"*

The stallion flashed by the stands, going faster with every magnificent stride. With a sudden spurt he bore down on Sun Raider. For a moment he hesitated as he came alongside. . . . Into the lead, the Black swept, past the cheering thousands—a step, a length, two lengths ahead—then the mighty giant plunged under the wire.

—*Walter Farley,* The Black Stallion

He uses his folly like a stalking horse.

—*William Shakespeare,* As You Like It, *Act V, Scene 4*

Ye old mule that think yourself so fair,
Leave off with craft your beauty to repair,
For it is true, without any fable,
No man setteth more by riding in your saddle.

—*Sir Thomas Wyatt*, "Ye Old Mule"

Mares, she said, had not been altered, in them the blood flowed freely, their life cycles had not been tampered with, their natures were completely their own. The mare usually had more energy than the gelding, could be as temperamental as the stallion and was, in fact, its superior.

—*John Hawkes*, Whistlejacket

The reeking, roaring hero of the chase,
I give him over as a desperate case.
Physicians write in hopes to work a cure,
Never, if honest ones, when death is sure;
And though the fox he follows may be tamed,
A mere fox-follower never is reclaim'd.
Some farrier should prescribe his proper course,
Whose only fit companion is his horse;
Or if, deserving of a better doom,
The noble beast judge otherwise, his groom.

—*William Cowper, "Conversations"*

The steeds soon perceived that the load they drew was lighter
than usual; and as a ship without ballast is tossed hither and thither
on the sea, so the chariot, without its accustomed weight, was dashed
as if empty.

—Bulfinch's Mythology, *"Phaeton"*

And that my Muse, to some ears not unsweet,
Tempers her words to trampling horses' feet
More oft than to a chamber melody.
        —*Sir Philip Sidney, "Astrophel and Stella, Sonnet VXXXIV"*

By the margin, willow veil'd,
Slide the heavy barges trail'd
By slow horses; and unhail'd.
                —*Alfred, Lord Tennyson, "The Lady of Shalott"*

Who drives the horses of the sun
Shall lord it but a day.
                —*John Vance Cheney, "The Happiest Heart"*

Meanwhile, impatient to mount and ride,
Booted and spurred, with a heavy stride
On the opposite shore walked Paul Revere.
Now he patted his horse's side,
Now he gazed at the landscape far and near,
Then, impetuous, stamped the earth,
And turned and tightened his saddle girth . . .
He springs to the saddle, the bridle he turns,
But lingers and gazes, till full on his sight
A second lamp in the belfry burns.
A hurry of hoofs in a village street,
A shape in the moonlight, a bulk in the dark,
And beneath, from the pebbles, in passing, a spark
Struck out by a steed flying fearless and fleet. . . .

—Henry Wadsworth Longfellow,
"The Midnight Ride of Paul Revere"

"I see nothing unusual," replied the king. "True, the mane is a handsome one. Yes, he is twice the size of the horses we keep here in the stables. His form is handsome, his eyes are bright. . . ."

"That is not all," interrupted the traveler. You have only to climb on his back and wish yourself anywhere in the world. And no matter how far the distance, in a flash of time too short to count you will find yourself there. It is this, Your Highness, that makes my horse so wonderful."

—Arabian Nights

The boy who rode on, slightly before him, sat a horse not only as if he'd been born to it—which he was—but as if, were he begot by malice or mischance into some queer land where horses never were, he would have found them anyway: would have known there was something missing for the world to be right, or he right in it, and would have set forth to wander wherever it was needed for as long as it took until he came upon one, and he would have known that that was what he sought, and it would have been.

—Cormac McCarthy, All the Pretty Horses

With his passion reverberating among the consonants like distant
thunder, he laid his hand upon the mane of his horse as though it had
been the gray locks of his adversary, swung himself into the saddle
and galloped away.

—*Bret Harte, "The Right Eye of the Commander"*

The Union's too big a horse to keep changing the saddle
Each time it pinches you, As long as you're sure
The saddle fits, you're bound to put up with the pinches
And not keep fussing the horse.

—*Stephen Vincent Benet, "John Brown's Body"*

The gemmy bridle glitter'd free,
Like to some branch of stars we see
Hung in the golden Galaxy.
The bridle bells rang merrily
As he rode down to Camelot . . .

—*Alfred, Lord Tennyson, "The Lady of Shallot"*

As two men ride of a horse, one must ride behind.

—*William Shakespeare,* Much Ado
About Nothing, *Act III, Scene 5*

What a piece of work is a horse! How noble in reason! How infinite in faculty! In form and moving how express and admirable! In action how like an angel! In apprehension how like a man! The beauty of the world! The paragon of animals!

—*James Agate, Alarums and Excursions*
[inspired by the "What a piece of work is man!"
speech from Shakespeare's Hamlet*]*

For many days we rode together,
Yet met we neither friend nor foe;
Hotter and clearer grew the weather,
Steadily did the East wind blow.

We saw the trees in the hot, bright weather,
Clear-cut, with shadows very black,
As freely we rode on together
With helms unlaced and bridles slack.

—*William Morris, "Riding Together"*

A groom used to spend whole days in currycombing and rubbing down his Horse, but at the same time stole his oats and sold them for his own profit. "Alas!" said the Horse, "if you really wish me to be in good condition, you should groom me less, and feed me more."

—*Aesop's Fables, "The Horse and the Groom"*

Her hooves fly faster than every flies the whirlwind,
Her tail-bone borne aloft, yet the hairs sweep the ground.
—*Anonymous Arabian poet, "The Ideal Horse"*

The tygers of wrath are wiser than the horses of instruction.
—*William Blake*, Songs of Innocence

You praise the firm restraint with which they write—
I'm with you there, of course:
They use the snaffle and the curb, all right,
But where's the bloody horse?
—*Roy Campbell, "On Some South African Novelists"*

[In the following exchange, Richard II, imprisoned after Henry Bolingbroke usurped the throne, is told by a groom that Brolingbroke rode the king's horse, Barbary, to Bolingbroke's coronation as King Henry IV]

King Richard: Rode he on Barbary? Tell me, gentle friend,
How went he under him?
Groom: So proudly as if he disdain'd the ground.
King Richard: So proud that Bolingbroke was on his back!
That jade hath eat bread from my royal hand;
This hand hath made him proud with clapping him.
Would he not stumble? Would he not fall down,
Since pride must have a fall, and break the neck
Of that proud man that did usurp his back?
Forgiveness, horse! Why do I rail on thee,
Since thou, created to be aw'd by man,
Wast born to bear? I was not made a horse;
And yet I bear a burden like an ass,
Spurr'd, gall'd and tir'd, by jauncing Bolingbroke.
                    —*William Shakespeare*, King Richard II,
                                        Act V, Scene 5

The truth is that horses exhibit, in an exaggerated form, many of the worst characteristics of people. They are greedy, envious, spiteful, malicious, slothful, superstitious, and stupid. They are congenital hysterics and each one is, ominously, a prospective homicide. If horses could talk, they would lie.
—*Owen Ulph*, The Fiddleback: Lore of the Line Camp

They were as fed horses in the morning: every one neighed after his neighbour's wife.
—*Bible, Jeremiah* 5:8.

I hear the Shadowy Horses, their long manes a-shake,
Their hoofs heavy with tumult, their eyes glimmering white. . . .
—*William Butler Yeats*, "He Bids His Beloved Be at Peace."

The white-crested fillies of the surge
And the white horses of the windy plain.
—*Roy Campbell*, Horses on the Camargue

So light to the croupe the fair lady he swung,
So light to the saddle before her he sprung!
"She is won! we are gone, over bank, bush, and scaur;
They'll have fleet steeds that follow," quoth young Lochinvar.
—*Sir Walter Scott, "Marmion"*

Lo! I knock the spurs away;
    Lo! I loosen belt and brand;
Hark! I hear the courser neigh
    For his stall in Fairy-land.
—*Winthrop Mackworth Praed, "Fairy Song"*

Edmund was absent at this time, or the evil would have been earlier remedied. When he returned, to understand how Fanny was situated, and perceived its ill effects, there seemed with him but one thing to be done; and that "Fanny must have a horse" was the resolute declaration with which he opposed whatever could be urged by the supineness of his mother, or the economy of his aunt, to make it appear unimportant. Mrs. Norris could not help thinking that some steady old thing might be found among the numbers belonging to the Park that would do vastly well; or that one might be borrowed of the steward; or that perhaps Dr. Grant might now and then lend them the pony he sent to the post. She could not but consider it as absolutely unnecessary, and even improper, that Fanny should have a regular lady's horse of her own, in the style of her cousins. She was sure Sir Thomas had never intended it: and she must say that, to be making such a purchase in his absence, and adding to the great expenses of his stable, at a time when a large part of his income was unsettled, seemed to her very unjustifiable. "Fanny must have a horse," was Edmund's only reply.

—*Jane Austen*, Mansfield Park

So long as a man rides his hobbyhorse peaceably and quietly along the king's highway, and neither compels you or me to get up behind him—pray, sir, what have you or I to do with it?

—*Laurence Sterne*, Tristam Shandy

The great advantage of a dialogue on horseback: it can be merged at any instant into a trot or canter, and one might escape from Socrates himself in the saddle.

—*George Eliot*, Adam Bede

What the horses o' Kansas think today, the horses of America will think tomorrow; and I tell you that when the horses of America rise in their might, the day o' the Oppressor is ended.

—*Rudyard Kipling*, The Day's Work

Now old Dunny was an outlaw, he'd grown so awful wild
He could paw the moon down, he could jump a mile;
Old Dunny stood right still there, like as he didn't know
Till the stranger had him saddled and ready for to go.
When the stranger hit the saddle, then old Dun he quit the earth,
And started travelin' upwards for all that he was worth,
A-yellin' and a-squealin' and a-having wall-eyed fits
His front feet perpendicular, his hind feet in the bits.

—*Cowboy song, "Zebra Dun"*

My love is a rider, wild broncos he breaks;
But he's promised to quit it soon just for my sake.
He ties one foot back and the saddle puts on;
With a swing and a jump, He is mounted and gone.

—*"My Love Is a Rider"*

Well, down in the horse corral standing alone,
Was that old cavayo, old Strawberry Roan,
His legs were spavined, and he had pigeon toes,
Little pig eyes and a big Roman nose . . .
Little pin ears that were crimped at the tip,
With a big 44 branded 'cross his left hip;
He's ewe-necked and old, with a long lower jaw,
You can see with one eye he's a reg'lar outlaw . . .
He went up towards the east and came down towards the west,
To stay in his middle I'm doin' my best,
He's about the worst bucker I've seen on the range
He can turn on a nickel and give you some change . . .
I turns over twice, and I comes back to earth
I lights in a-cussin' the day of his birth
I know there is ponies I'm unable to ride
Some are still living, they haven't all died.

                    —*Cowboy song, "Strawberry Roan"*

Oh, for a ride o'er the prairies free,
  On a fiery untamed steed,
  Where the curlews fly and the coyotes cry
  And the western wind goes sweeping by,
  For my heart enjoys the speed.

With my left hand light on the bridle rein,
  And the saddle girth pinched behind,
  With the lariat tied at the pony's side
  By my stout right arm that's true and tried,
We race with the whistling wind.

—*"The Cowboys Ride"*

My beautiful! my beautiful!
  That standeth meekly by
With thy proudly arch'd and glossy neck,
  And dark and fiery eye;
The stranger hath they bridle-rein,
  Thy master hath his gold;
Fleet limbed and beautiful, farewell;
  Thou'rt sold; my steed, thou'rt sold.

—*Caroline Elizabeth Sheridan Norton,*
  "The Arab's Farewell to His Steed"

IV

RIDING

AND

TRAINING

If the art were not so difficult we would have plenty of good riders and excellently ridden horses, but as it is the art requires, in addition to everything else, character traits that are not combined in everyone: inexhaustible patience, firm perseverance under stress, courage combined with quiet alertness. If the seed is present only a true, deep love for the horse can develop these character traits to the height that alone will lead to the goal.

—*Gustav Steinbrecht*

A horse is the matter and subject whereupon the art worketh, and is a creature sensible, and therefore so far as he is moved to do anything, he is thereunto moved by sense and feeling. Further, this is common to all sensible creatures, to shun all things as annoy them, and to like all such things as do delight them.

—*John Astley*, The Art of Riding

All horses are wild and skittish when unsure hands touch them.

—*Clarice Lispector, "Dry Point of Horses"*

It is the seat on a horse that makes the difference between a groom and a gentleman.

—*Miguel de Cervantes*, Don Quixote

"Tricks" have no place in the art of riding, since in moments of crisis, when effective action is most needed, the superficial "trick" never succeeds.

—*Lt. Col. A.L. d'Endrody*, Give Your Horse a Chance

"The great art of riding, as I was saying, is to keep your balance properly. Like this, you know—" He let go the bridle and stretched out both his arms to show Alice what he meant, and this time he fell flat on his back, right under the horse's feet.

"Plenty of practice!" he went on repeating, all the time that Alice was getting him on his feet again.

—*Lewis Carroll*, Alice Through the Looking Glass

No time spent in the saddle is wasted; as you learn to communicate with the horse and appreciate what he can do for you, it will add a fascinating dimension to your life.

—*Mary Gordon-Watson*, The Handbook of Riding

Ride your horse as you feel him, provided you were born to, or over the years have learned to feel! It is the one thing no book can teach you, no teacher can give you, the one conquest of the laurels which will be entirely yours.

—*Jean Froissard*, Classical Horsemanship for Our Time

Keep one leg on one side, the other leg on the other side, and your mind in the middle.

—*Henry Taylor*

A good seat on a horse steals away your opponent's courage and
your onlooker's heart—what reason is there to attack? Sit like one
who has conquered.

—Friedrich Nietzsche

Equitation is not the search for public acclaim and self satisfaction
after applause. Nor is it the pleasure of every prize or a judge or jury's
admiration at a show. It is the head to head dialogue with the horse
and the search for communication and perfection.

—Nuno Oliveira

A horse has no future. It cannot greet the sun and say today will be
better. It can only reflect upon days of past experiences. It is our job
to create a positive past.

—Karen West

Love animals. God has given them the rudiments of thought and joy untroubled. Do not trouble their joy, do not harass them, do not deprive them of their happiness, do not work against God's intention.

—*Fyodor Dostoyevsky*, The Brothers Karamazov

Viscount d'Abzac, when he was eighty years old, said that he learned again every day. Baucher's quest, by having never reached an end, testified that as great as his talent was in the training of his horses, despite the fact that they presented great perfection, they did not give complete satisfaction to the master. His feeling revealed to him yet a higher perfection. One day I said to Baucher that he would never be completely satisfied with the training of my horses. He replied to me: "But it will be always so and thus always there is something remaining to desire."

—*General Alexis L'Hotte*

A horse dealer and his son went to look at a horse for sale. The father asked his son to get on one of the horses. The son turned to his father and asked, "Shall I ride the horse as if I am selling it or as if I am buying it?"

—*Source unknown*

A good horseman trains his horses to go his way. A great horseman rides his horses the way they want to be ridden.

—*Barbara Worth*

Treat a horse like a woman and a woman like a horse. And they'll both win for you.

—*Elizabeth Arden*

Get your tack and equipment just right, and then forget about it and concentrate on the horse and your ride.

—*William Steinkraus*

Horses are not tamed by whips or blows. The strength of ten men is not so strong as a single strike of the hoof; the experience of ten men is not enough, for this is the unexpected, the unpredictable.

—*Beryl Markham*

A good cowboy will make whatever he's riding better—and a poor cowboy will be afoot even on a good horse.

—*Ray Hunt*

There are some people who, as soon as they get on a horse, entirely undressed and untaught, fancy that by beating and spurring they will make him a dressed horse in one morning only. I would fain ask such stupid people whether by beating a boy they would teach him to read without first showing him the alphabet? Sure, they would beat him to death, before they would make him read.

—*William Cavendish, Duke of Newcastle*

Thou must learn the thoughts of the noble horse
Whom thou wouldst ride.
Be not indiscreet in thy demands,
Nor require him to perform indiscreetly.

—*Johanne Wolfgang von Goethe*

The way you start a colt is critical. Once [Tom Dorrance] taught us to be softer, kinder, gentler, our horses worked better. It actually makes a difference when a horse likes you.

—*Greg Ward*

If you have a problem getting along with neighbors or people in school, you might as well forget about training horses. Training horses is not fighting with them. And it's not a business for a person who is lazy. It takes a lot of drive.

—*Marvin Mayfield*

It lies in the hands of every single rider whether horse and rider feel relaxed. It must be every rider's supreme aim to create relaxation of mind and body.

—*Klaus Balkenhol*

. . . and he whispered to the horse, trust no man in whose eyes you do not see yourself reflected as an equal.

—*Source unknown*

~

There is nothing in which a horse's power is better revealed than in a neat, clean stop.

—*Michel de Montaigne*

~

To expect to ride without encountering difficulties and worries, as well as risks and dangers, is only to look for something that cannot possibly be attained.

—Riding for Ladies, *1887*

~

There's a variety of horse minds as big as there is among human minds. Some need more pursuading than others, and a few of 'em, no matter how firm they're handled, will have to be showed again and again that they can't get away with this or that.

—*Will James*, Smoky the Cowhorse

Practice sharpens, but overschooling blunts the edge. If your horse isn't doing right, the first place to look is yourself.

—*Joe Heim, quoted in Barbara Schulte,*
Cutting, One Run at a Time

At its finest, rider and horse are joined not by tack, but by trust. Each is totally reliant upon the other. Each is the selfless guardian of the other's very well-being.

—*Source unknown*

The horse you get off is not the same as the horse you got on. It is your job as a rider to ensure that as often as possible, the change is for the better.

—*Source unknown*

There is a way to train a horse where when you get done you've got the horse. On his own ground. A good horse will figure things out on his own. You can see what's in his heart.

—*Cormac McCarthy*, Cities of the Plain

Just grab tight with your knees and keep your hands away from the saddle, and if you get throwed, don't let that stop you. No matter how good a man is, there's always some horse can pitch him. You just climb up again before he gets to feeling smart about it. Pretty soon, he won't throw you no more, and pretty soon he can't throw you no more.

—*John Steinbeck*, The Red Pony

The main thing to remember about horsemanship is that is a physical art. If a man runs well, it is probably due to the fact that he was born with good legs and wind and has been able to keep himself fit. If a man rides well, it is probably due to the same reason.

—Paul T. Albert

Horses can be scary animals to work with, due to their size and apparent skittishness, but often fear of an animal is just covering up other personal issues that the person is trying to deal with. I've never seen a situation where a person was just simply afraid of their horse, and didn't have that same characteristic fear permeating their entire life fabric. It always does. I guess because horses are larger and more powerful than we are, working with them can be a very revealing time for the owner—any fear that was there to start with is greatly magnified. And I don't know anyone who wants the things below the surface of their psyches to be revealed publicly. Surprise! Around horses, it all comes to the surface.

—Buck Brannaman

There never was a rider so smart that some horse could not teach him a new trick. Because of this, horsemanship and horse training is a lifelong study.

—*Paul T. Albert*

If you are going to teach a horse something and have a good relationship, you don't make him learn it—you let him learn it.

—*Ray Hunt*

Remember, a horse can tell you a lot of things, if you watch, and expect it to be sensible and intelligent.

—*Mary O'Hara*

Remember that an easy hand is one of the principal aids we have; for it puts a horse upon its haunches, when he finds nothing else to lean upon; besides, it pleases him, and prevents his being resty.

—*William Cavendish, Duke of Newcastle*

Time and patience are required of all good horsemen, so hurry when you are not around your horse.

—*Bob Denhardt*

It takes no more time and effort to train and finish out a good looking horse than a poor looking one.

—*Dick Spencer III*

To the mistress who thoroughly understands the art of managing [horses], the horse gives his entire affection and obedience, becomes her most willing slave, submits to all her whims, and is proud and happy under her rule.

—The American Horsewoman, *1884*

Progression in the schooling of the horse must, quite definitely, be graduated, because gradual progress is the main road to success. If on a given day, an unexpected improvement has been achieved, it should not be taken as something that has been definitely acquired and should not be taken as a basis for the lesson of the following day. If one did so, one would most surely be disappointed.

—*General Alexis L'Hotte*

When training his horse, the rider must repeat over and over again, "I have time."

—*Alois Podhajsky*

The Pacific Ocean is off to your left. The Atlantic Ocean is off to your right. Your horse has got to stop sometime.

—*Montana horseman to a visitor worried about being run away with*

The horse will leap over trenches, will jump out of them, will do anything else, provided one grants him praise and respite after his accomplishment.

—*Xenophon*

There are only two emotions that belong in the saddle; one is a sense of humor and the other is patience.

—*John Lyons*

If you act like you've only got fifteen minutes, it'll take all day. Act like you've got all day and it'll take fifteen minutes.

—*Monty Roberts*

With easy seat behold them ride—
These are the Truly qualified—
Models of Sporting Men;
Graceful and elegant, yet neat;
Egad, the very sight's a treat
I long to have again!

—*Source unknown*

Spoiled horses, difficult horses, and even rogues, can teach us much that is important; the rider who is too well mounted may never really learn to ride.

—*William C. Steinkraus*, Riding and Jumping

. . . It is also good to pet the beast while he eats so that he will relax.

—*Marcus Aurelius*

A horse can be made to do almost anything if his master has intelligence enough to let him know what is required.

—*Ulysses S. Grant*

The first and most important basic is a good attitude toward the horse. I know that many of us were taught that we must "master" the horse, and be the boss, but while I don't believe in spoiling horses, I do feel that this kind of thinking is as outdated as women automatically being submissive to men or children being seen and not heard. The results of allowing the horse to tell you when you are wrong (as long as he doesn't tell you in an aggressive way) are astounding and rewarding for everyone.

—*Gincy Self Bucklin*, How Your
Horse Wants You to Ride

If a rider's heart is in the right place, his seat will be independent of his hands.

—*Piero Santini*

The school horse is a very important, almost indispensable assistant to the instructor. But he will be of full value only if the instructor is thoroughly acquainted with his movements and his temperament. . . . When the instructor has not trained the horse himself, he should ride the horse before starting to train his pupil in order to get to know his capabilities.

—*Alois Podhajsky*, My Horses, My Teachers

The shoulder-in is the aspirin of equitation; it cures everything.

—*Nuno Oliveira*

"Dancing and riding, it's the same damn thing," he would say. "It's about trust and consent. You've gotten hold of one another. The man's leading but he's not dragging her, he's offering a feel and she feels it and goes with him. You're in harmony and moving to each other's rhythm, just follow the feel."

—*Nicholas Evans*, The Horse Whisperer

Before you swing a leg over a horse, you should know why you're swinging it.

—*Marlene McRae*

A good rider can feel his way into a horse very quickly. He knows what a horse needs. He must establish harmony between horse and rider. He must not wait for the horse to do this. How much or how little of an aid does a horse need? How can he teach this horse to respond to lighter aids? How can he motivate this horse? The good rider quickly gains the trust and confidence of the horse, because the horse understands his aids.

—*Ernst Hoyos, in* Dressage Masters *by David Collins*

I once gave Eugen Herrigel's little masterpiece *Zen in the Art of Archery* to Buster [Western trainer Buster Welch] to read and he concluded that its application to horsemanship was that if you are thinking about your riding you are interfering with your horse.

—*Thomas McGuane, "Buster"*

Hardly any feeling is more distressing than the certain knowledge that you and your horse are about to part company, and it's remarkable how threatening even the softest, grassiest turf suddenly begins to look when you realize you're about to hit it hard, head— (or shoulder—) first.

—*Michael Korda*, Horse People

You can think your way out of many problems faster than you can ride your way out of them.

—*William Steinkraus*, Riding and Jumping

. . . patience, inexhaustible patience—especially when psychological and physical defects are present—is necessary to make the horse understand what we want of it. Patience is equally necessary in order not to grow immoderately demanding, which always happens when we do not reward an initial compliance by immediate cessation of the demand, but try to enjoy a victory until the horse becomes cross or confused.

—*Waldemar Seunig*, Horsemanship

The horse doesn't understand the difference between right and wrong. He only understands in terms of what is. If I kick and he does a behavior after that, whatever that behavior is, he thinks that's what he's supposed to do. He doesn't think in terms of this is right behavior and this is wrong behavior.

—John Lyons

To learn all that a horse could teach, was a world of knowledge, but only a beginning. . . .

Look into a horses eye and you instantly know if you can trust him.

—Mary O'Hara

If training has not made a horse more beautiful, nobler in carriage, more attentive in his behavior, revealing pleasure in his own accomplishment . . . then he has not truly been schooled in dressage.

—Colonel Hans Handler

Experienced riders are not prone to brag. And usually newcomers, if they start out being boastful, end up modest.

—*C. J. J. Mullen*

Let Me Teach You

When you are tense, let me teach you to relax.
When you are short tempered, let me teach you to be patient.
When you are short sighted, let me teach you to see.
When you are quick to react, let me teach you to be thoughtful.
When you are angry, let me teach you to be serene.
When you feel superior, let me teach you be respectful.
When you are self-absorbed, let me teach you to think of
    greater things.
When you are arrogant, let me teach you humility.
When you are lonely, let me be your companion.
When you are tired, let me carry the load.
When you need to learn, let me teach you.
After all, I am your horse.

—*Source unknown*

You want to do as little as possible but as much as it takes.

—*Buck Brannaman, on achieving results in training*

A horse doesn't care how much you know until he knows how
much you care.

—*Pat Parelli*

A man of kindness to his horse, is kind
But brutal actions show a brutal mind.
He was designed thy servant, not thy drudge.
Remember his creator is thy judge.

—*Source unknown*

It is the difficult horses that have the most to give you.

—*Lendon Gray*

Every time you ride, you're either teaching or un-teaching your horse.

—*Gordon Wright*

You cannot train a horse with shouts and expect it to obey a whisper.

—*Dagobert D. Runes*

Dressage lessons in the manège, by reason of their constraints on the horse, must be of short duration and the horse must return to the stable in as happy a frame of mind as when he left it.

—*General Alexis L'Hotte*

If anybody expects to calm a horse down by tiring him out with riding swiftly and far, his supposition is the reverse of the truth.

—*Xenophon*

In training horses, one trains himself.

—*Antoine De Pluvinet*

A horse is like a violin, first it must be tuned, and when tuned it must be accurately played.

—*Source unknown*

Riders who force their horses by the use of the whip only increase their fear for they then associate the pain with the thing that frightens them.

—*Xenophon*

How do you get a horse to be curious? You've got to have not approach and retreat, but retreat. Why do horses get porcupine quills in their noses? Because the thing waddles away from them. This is what causes curiosity: Things that go away and waddle and have a curious manner.

—*Pat Parelli*

We dominate a horse by mind over matter. We could never do it by brute strength.

—*Monica Dickens*

Even the greenest horse has something to teach the wisest rider.

—*Source unknown*

Nothing on four legs is quicker than a horse heading back
to the barn.

—*Source unknown*

In training there is always the tendency to proceed too rapidly;
go slowly with careful, cautious steps. Make frequent demands;
be content with little; be lavish in rewards.

—*General Faverot de Kerbrech*

The only approbation a rider should covet is that of his horse.

—*E. Beudant*

There are many types of bits for many different disciplines, but the
severity of all bits lies in the hands holding them.

—*Monte Roberts*

Whenever difficulties appear, the rider must ask himself: does the horse not want to execute my demands, does he not understand what I want, or is he physically unable to carry them out? The rider's conscience must find the answer.

—*Alois Podhajsky*

Then there was the bridle. Billy explained how to use a stick of licorice for a bit until Galiban was used to having something in his mouth. Billy explained, "Of course we could force-break him to everything, but he wouldn't be as good a horse if we did. He'd always be a bit afraid, and he wouldn't mind because he wanted to."

—*John Steinbeck*, THE RED PONY

The horse thinks one thing and he who saddles him another.

—*Benjamin Franklin*

A young trooper should have an old horse.

—*H. G. Bohn*

Let the best horse leap the hedge first.

—Thomas Fuller

If the horse does not enjoy his work, his rider will have no joy.

—H. H. Isenbart

Horses have as much individuality and character as people.

—C. W. Anderson

There ain't a horse that can't be rode; there ain't a man that can't
be throwed.

—Cowboy saying

The two outstanding memories in the animal kingdom are the elephant and the horse. In the case of the horse, you have to remember when to run in order to stay alive. So horses have a phenomenal memory and there's no time lapse. They memorize something that impresses them, good or bad, and ten years goes by, it's still there.

—*Dr. Robert Miller*

Falling off is sometimes dangerous, occasionally fatal, and always humiliating. In all my years of taking riding lessons I was so determined never to fall off that I never did; even the times I should have, my instructor would look over to see the spectacle of a man half out of the saddle defying the force of gravity by clutching his horse's mane with grim determination.

—*Stephen Budiansky, "Tallyho and Tribulation"*

Beauty, delicacy and position—these were the foundations of courtly equestrianism.

—*Henning Eichberg*

Ask often, be content of little, reward always.

—*Captain Etienne Beudant*

A ruthlessly condensed training only leads to a general superficiality, to travesties of the movements, and to a premature unsoundness of the horse. Nature cannot be violated.

—*Colonel Alexis Podjalsky*

The trot is the foundation of the gallop.

—*Richard Berenger*

The horse has such a docile nature, that he would always rather do right than wrong, if he can only be taught to distinguish one from the other.

—*George Melville*

If your horse says no, you either asked the wrong question, or asked the question wrong.

—*Pat Parelli*

If you start getting nervous about getting hurt you will be. . . . If you are worrying about the danger it's time to give up.

—*Jason Weaver, jockey*

No gymnastics could be better or harder exercise, and this and the art of riding, are of all the arts the most befitting a free man.

—*Plato, Laches*

You can't control a young horse unless you can control yourself.

—*Lincoln Steffans*, The Autobiography of Lincoln Steffans

The one best precept—the golden rule in dealing with a horse—is never to approach him angrily. Anger is so deviod of forethought that it will often drive a man to do things which in a calmer mood he will regret.

—Xenophon

I remember one of the foremost princes of France, who took his son to M. Duplessis, who was already the most distinguished of the famous ecuyers that I have mentioned. I remember, I said, how the prince told him as he approached him: "I am not bringing you my son to make him an ecuyer. I simply want you to teach him to coordinate his legs and hands with the thought in mind of what he wants his horse to do."

M. Duplessis answered him in my presence, as I had the honor of being one of his disciples: "Sire, it has been close to sixty years that I have been working towards learning what you have given me the honor of telling me. And here you want me to teach him all that I hope to accomplish myself."

—Gaspard de Saunier

Even though teaching is a wordy enterprise, the business of being on a horse is not. Henry Wynmalen faces this problem honestly by invoking poetry: "It is true that one must, in teaching riding, try to explain to students the nature and manner of the aids one uses, and to a certain extent this can be done," he says. "But only to a limited extent. . . . The same word, in poetry as in prose, can have many intonations and many meanings. Just so in riding, where the same aid can be given an almost infinity of meanings and intonations, whereby in the end a veritable language, and a reciprocal one, comes into being between horse and rider."

—*Helen Husher,* Conversations with a Prince

Oh, those school stallions—there is no end to stories and anecdotes about them. I have certainly learned to respect their personalities and to acknowledge them as teachers. On the other hand they become teachers only when the rider endeavours to understand their reactions and their behaviour. Since they cannot speak they are limited to signals. Perhaps many a rider may even be called lucky that they are unable to speak because they would often have occasion to put in complaints about incomprehension, ignorance, impatience, injustice, and ingratitude. Instead they serve man in silent and irrevocable loyalty.

—*Colonel Alois Podhajskey, "School Horses"*

One of the most important aspects of the true horseman is his "horsemanlike" attitude, which is expressed in his thinking, in his conduct, and the way he presents his horses, his facility, and himself. Perhaps the best word for the attitude is "respect": respect for the horse—*any* horse—as a living creature; respect for other people, in and out of the horse world . . . respect for hard work; respect for himself.

—*Susan Harris, in George H. Morris,*
The American Jumping Style

At any rate, if we ever lose our calm and cannot promptly regain it, we had better leave the school and go for a hack, or else alight and return the horse to the stables. It won't be wasted time; at worst no progress is being made that day, but at least we have made no retrograde steps in our relationship with our horse.

—*Jean Froissard,* Classical Horsemanship for Our Time

It's your responsibility when you start working with a troubled horse to set specific behavioral boundaries. It is at this point in a horse's life that we humans have an opportunity to show just how evolved we are. We can help the horse focus on constructive tasks that ease his fears and show him that he's not alone in this world of predators.

—*Buck Brannaman,* The Faraway Horses

Horse sense is actually the animal's instinct for self preservation. . . .
To the horse, reward is the lack of punishment, in other words, self
preservation. The horse is one of the most timid of animals physically and is easily frightened by rough handling or an unfortunate
experience. There is no such thing as a horse who is not afraid.

—*Gordon Wright*, Horsemanship

Beware of the horse-as-machine approach to riding and training:
"There's a gadget for every problem," a new bit (or martingale) will
fix that horse." Beware of anyone whose only approach to problem-
solving involves adding more equipment or more severe hardware.
Equipment problems . . . can and should be solved with different
equipment. Training problems, on the other hand, cannot and should
not be dealt with on a mechanical basis.

—*Jessica Jahiel*, Riding for the Rest of Us

If there is one rule to follow when it comes to training horses, it is
this: there are no hard and fast rules!

—*Dave Kelley*

The problem I see people having with their horses is due to so many
of them thinking they can start out quite a ways up the line from
where the horse is in his development. Some real important things
get passed over when they start way up there. To get the better
results, a person needs to start down below where most people want
to work with the horse.

—*Bill Dorrance,* True Horsemanship Through Feel

A trainer has to be observant. He has to watch the horses and figure
out what they are thinking. This requires a feel for horses. This feel
is directly connected to passion. There is a relationship between
passion and feel, just as there is between respect and friendship.
A rider that uses his horse like a tool has no respect for horses and
no love. He is not a friend of the horse. This rider will never learn to
dance with horses.

—*George Theodorescu, in* Dressage Masters, *by David Collins*

An extra pressure, a silent rebuke, an unseen praising, a firm correction: all these passed between us as through telegraph wires.

—*Christilot Hanson Boylen*

The horse does not execute down transitions by pulling the forehand backwards, but by stepping under with his hind legs.

—*E. F. Seidler*

It has been able to judge the rider's good nature by the fact that he was on the lookout, so to speak, for the slightest indication of responsiveness to his controls to find an opportunity to reward his horse, and that he was magnanimous in forgetting to punish when the mistake was due to clumsiness or inadequate understanding.

—*Waldemar Seunig*

Riding is a partnership. The horse lends you his strength, speed and grace, which are greater than yours. For your part you give him your guidance, intelligence and understanding, which are greater than his. Together you can achieve a richness that alone neither can.

—Lucy Rees

The hardest thing to do on a horse is nothing at all.

—Source unknown

Great riders are not great because of their talent; they are great because of their passion.

—Source unknown

You only need two things to ride a horse. Confidence and balance. Everything else you can pick up as you go along.

—Allan D. Keating

Your legs are a horse's courage.

—*Source unknown*

The rider has to be carried by the horse and to give him the best, the most conducive posture for carrying and going. The rider's role is thus an active one, in so far as he has to establish and to maintain this posture and this gait. Once he has succeeded in this respect, his role is a passive one in so far as he has to do nothing else than to avoid interfering with his horse and to make the task of carrying and going as pleasant as possible for him.

—*Gustav von Dreyhausen*

But if a rider teach his horse to go with the bridle loose . . . he would thus lead him to do everything in . . . pleasure and pride.

—*John Astley*

The horse knows how to be a horse if we will leave him alone . . .
but the riders don't know how to ride. What we should be doing is
creating riders and that takes care of the horse immediately.

—*Charles de Kunffy*

We shall take great care not to annoy the horse and spoil his
friendly charm, for it is like the scent of a blossom—once lost it
will never return.

—*Pluvinel*

In order to excel at an art it is not enough to know the principles and
to have practiced them for a long time. It is also necessary to be able
to choose wisely the subjects that are capable of executing these
principles. This is what constitutes mainly the skill of the masters
and the perfection of the disciples. It is also what most riders neglect.
Out of presumptuousness or ignorance, they try unsuccessfully and
flatter themselves in vain to train indiscriminately all horses they
encounter, as if nature had created all animals equal and destined
them for the same usage.

—*Gaspard de Saunier*

When you're learning to get with your horse, you're also learning about what there is to see. I sometimes think about when you look over on that hill there, why you may not see anything the first time you look. But you keep looking and you're liable to pick up something that you didn't see the first time. It's like that with the horse.

—*Bill Dorrance*, True Horsemanship Through Feel

Some people think horses are dumb. Ability and intelligence are in all horses, regardless of breed. Their so-called stupidity stems from our poor communication. Training a horse is like drawing a picture. The better I draw the picture, the better the communication. If I'm drawing a horse in pencil, I've communicated something. If I add crayon to my drawing, you can then tell that the horse I've drawn is a Palomino. Does that mean that you've gotten smarter? No. It means that I've become a better communicator.

—*John Lyons*, Lyons on Horses

When riding a high-strung horse, pretend you are riding an old one.

—*Dominique Barbier*, Souvenirs

As one of the famous d'Inzeo brothers, riders on the Italian jumping team at the Rome Olympics, was quoted as saying, "The mastery of a perfect technique takes a lifetime. Technical mastery is merely sufficient for you to become good; it is not enough to make you great. From excellence to greatness, a man is alone. He must count on imponderables—his own instinctive resources, his character and his secret gifts. They are never the same for two people, not even for brothers."

> —*Michael O. Page, in* The U.S. Equestrian Team Book of Riding, *edited by William Steinkraus*

What does it take to train a horse? More time than the horse has.

> —*Larry Mahan, former all-around rodeo champion*

What is it that makes horses give their rider everything? It can only be a reaction based on mutual trust. Once a horse trusts his partner, he develops and grows; and once a rider has found trust in his horse's abilities, he can develop the confidence needed to achieve special accomplishments.

> —*Elizabeth Furst,* Visions of Show Jumping

Many riding accidents would never have happened if people could control the false pride that makes them almost ashamed to ask for a quiet horse. But a good horseman can get anything he wants out of any horse, and I have never been able to figure out the illogic that makes poor riders think that they can control a high-spirited horse when, by their own admission, they can't even make the quiet horse move forward!

—*Gordon Wright*, Learning to Ride, Hunt, and Show

Learning about our horses is learning about ourselves as well, seeing how our personalities mesh or clash with the horses we choose to ride or train.

—*Linda Tellington-Jones*, Getting in Touch: Understand and Influence Your Horse's Personality

A rider's total belief in an instructor is, of course, another
essential. When students doubt me a little, I suggest other
teachers they should go to. Without belief, discipline is a
mockery, if not downright impossible.

> —*George H. Morris*, George H. Morris
> Teaches Beginners to Ride

Everyone who wants justly to call himself—or herself—a rider
should ponder the following statement very seriously: 99 percent
of all horses have quite a number of bad habits which are commonly
put down to disobedience. And 99 percent of all riders do not
understand how to break their horses of such habits.

> —*Wilhelm Müsler*, Riding Logic

A real horseman must not only be an expert—he must also be able
to think and feel like a horse, that is, to realize that a horse is not
equipped with human understanding. Such a horseman should
be both horse and man—a centaur, not only physically, but also
psychologically—anthropomorphic and hippomorphic.

> *Waldemar Seunig*, Horsemanship

Nanticoke [a show jumper of the 1960s] reinforced a lesson I'd already started to learn from other horses: never try to muscle your way with a horse. There may or may not be an ideal way to do things, but in the horse world you have to be realistic, willing to try different solutions to a problem until you find one that works both for you and the horse. Letting Naticoke jog along while I mounted wasn't ideal, but it was good horsemanship because we started the ride relaxed instead of with a fight.

—*Rodney Jenkins, in* Practical Horseman's Book of Riding, Training, & Showing Hunters & Jumpers *edited by M. A. Stoneridge*

Do not demand at the end of the lesson what the horse cannot do easily and happily yet! Always finish the lesson with something the horse is able to do easily and that he will thus perform happily, so that there is cause for praise and display of affection.

—*Peter Spohr*

V

THE HORSE

IN

SPORT

SHOWING

You win, you're happy; you lose, you're disappointed—but don't let either one carry you away.

—Buster Welch

If riding were all blue ribbons and bright lights, I would have quit long ago.

—George Morris

Horse shows are the one form of competition where it really matters how you play the game, not if you win or lose.

—Daniel Lenehan, in Harlan C. Abbey,
Showing Your Horse

Ride 'em and slide 'em.

—*Reining in a nutshell*

Feed 'em and lead 'em.

—*Conformation classes in a nutshell*

Two words not commonly related to winning or losing at the horse show ring correlate to the color of the ribbons received. The two words are "act" and "react." Winners act. Nonwinners react.

—*Don Burt*, Winning with the American Quarter Horse

There are a million miles of difference between the words "win" and "beat." We don't even allow the word "beat" on this farm. Because when you start talking about beating someone, you've lost your concentration. You're thinking about the opposition.

—*Helen Crabtree*

As any parent knows, raising children is a complex and expensive process. Raising a child who loves horses brings greater complexity and expense to the arena (no pun intended). Going forward in this millennium, we are faced with rapid-fire changes in technology that are constantly affecting our lives and our lifestyles. And for all the so-called ease of life that advanced technology is supposed to bring, we constantly find ourselves more hurried, more harried, over-worked, and tired. As parents, when our child loves horses, we are first taken aback and then pleased on some deep subliminal level that our child has dragged us into this world where time has stopped and the language becomes one of smells and whinnies and warmth.

—*Susan Daniels,* The Horse Show
Mom's Survival Guide

The criminal trial today is . . . a kind of show-jumping contest in which the rider for the prosecution must clear every obstacle to succeed.

—*Robert Mark, Commissioner, London Metropolitan Police*

When I was a child, I used to jump bareback over fences four to four and a half feet high. I don't remember being afraid. I think my mother took custody of the fear for me, and my job was only not to fall off and not to let on how often I was jumping. When I came back to riding at forty-four, though, every little two-foot fence looked to me like a Puissance wall.

—*Jane Smiley*

The rider's judgment and communication with his horse and the horse's confidence in the rider should be so highly developed that they are in harmony. What separates the good from the not-so-good and the bad is not the size of the jumps but the combination of horse and rider. The best combination should win.

—*Bertalan de Némethy*

An exhibitor went up to a horse show judge to complain about being placed below someone who made some sort of mistake, such as being on the wrong lead. The judge's explanation: "The other guy did it better wrong than you did it right."

—*Source unknown*

A horse which stops dead just before a jump and thus propels its rider into a graceful arc provides a splendid excuse for general merriment.

—*Prince Philip, Duke of Edinburgh*

In the language of the range, to say that somebody is "as smart as a cutting horse" is to say that he is smarter than a Philadelphia lawyer, smarter than a steel trap, smarter than a coyote, smarter than a Harvard graduate—all combined. There just can't be anything smarter than a smart cutting horse. He can do everything but talk Meskin—and he understands that.

—*Joe M. Evans*, A Corral Full of Stories

In practice do things as perfectly as you can; in competition, do what you have to do.

—*William Steinkraus*, Riding and Jumping

Had I but known about breathing in my youth, how much simpler my competitive riding life would have been.

—Victor Hugo-Vidal, in Showing for Beginners
by Halley I. McEvoy

One matinee Gordon Wright was showing a jumper at the National Horse Show. He had just had one of his books published, and when his horse stopped at a fence, [jumper rider] Joe Green, who had a voice that could carry, yelled from the in gate, "Hey, Gordon, what chapter is that in?!"

—Clarence "Honey" Craven

We look for a "been there, done that" kind of horse. Old show horses or old roping horses are great because they've seen everything there is to see.

—Ann Larson

Half the failures in life arise from pulling in one's horse as he is leaping.

—*Julius and Augustus Hare*

∽

I truthfully think a show horse has a very easy life. When I'm hot, no one gives me a bath, I have to bathe myself. If I'm hungry, I have to feed myself, no one does it for me. When my legs are sore, no one rubs them for me. What I'm saying, then, is that if you feed a horse well, groom him well, have a clean comfortable stall for him, and take care of him when he's hurt, the least he should do is what you want him to—and all you usually want him to do is jump a fence.

—*Rodney Jenkins, in Harlan C. Abbey,* Showing Your Horse

∽

A cutting competition is nothing more than a contest of "oh shits" and "attaboys." And the person with more attaboys is the winner.
                        —*Buster Welch, quoted in Lynn Campion,*
        Training and Showing the Cutting Horse

[Show jumper] Uncle Max came out of the Cowtown Rodeo in New Jersey where he was a saddle bronc. He always remembered that when the saddle was put on and the girth tightened—his job was to get the rider off. Getting on was always a problem. There were times I had to take flying leaps to get into the saddle or drop down from a car hood or roof or even drop down from the hayloft of a barn while Max was led underneath. He wasn't a mean horse or was he difficult to ride once you got on—it was all show, but he put on quite a show in the schooling area and going into the ring.
        —*Neal Shapiro, quoted in* The U.S. Equestrian Team
            Book of Riding, *edited by William C. Steinkraus*

DRESSAGE

If the horse is used for the purpose of the rider's ego in winning competition points, dressage is no longer an art but an abuse of a generous long-suffering animal.

—*Sally O'Connor*

As with many concepts in riding, the principles at the beginning and advanced levels are basically the same; they just become more refined as one progresses. Riding a horse becomes more like conducting an orchestra. Each instrument must be played individually before they can be played together in concert. . . . When all of this functions according to plan, the rider plays the horse between the aids. The result is a happy, rhythmic horse.

—*David Collins*

Dressage competition should be some fun, particularly in the lower levels. You are perfectly entitled to smile at the mishaps of your competitors if you can just as easily laugh at yourself and your own misfortunes. Put in perspective, all you have to do is induce your horse to show his best side for five minutes in front of the judge.

—*Max Gahwyler*

One of the most beautiful things is when you train a young horse and bring him up to Grand Prix. I have done this many times. That is really something beautiful. It is really a victory. It is more than a competition victory. It is an inner contentment that I get when I know that I have accomplished my work.

—*Ernst Hoyos, quoted in* Dressage Masters, *by David Collins*

Lendon [Gray] listens to all kinds of horses. She is a democrat.
In the dressage world, where big horses with extravagant movement
have created the standard, this makes her an iconoclast. She rides
some of these big horses, but just as often she rides diminutive Arabs,
quarter horses, Morgans, ponies of various descriptions. She rides
horses that have been schooled for the jumping arena, ex-racehorses,
cutting horses, and once she brought out a horse that had been
trained for the sole purpose of dog and pony shows. She believes
in the process of dressage, that it will make even the most homely
unaccomplished animal more beautiful and capable. In her hands,
this is what happens. One of her clients has a small gray Arabian.
On a summer weekend Lendon showed the horse in lower-level
dressage and won the division. Two weeks later, she reported with
great pride, the horse's owner, an endurance rider, won a hundred-
mile competitive trail ride with him.

—*Holly Menino, "The Ponies Are Talking"*

Some competitors buy very advanced horses, then drop them down
into Training Level, which is obvious to any experienced observer. I
consider this practice to be unfair to the other competitors, and one
that should not rate very high with judges. . . . But after a while, even
these horses regress to the level of their riders. No horse stays better
than the rider on his back for very long.

—*Max Gahwayler*

A competition rider should possess a moral maturity. He should
be mature enough to be able to form an understanding, a working
relationship with the creature, the horse. He should never treat
his horse as a mechanical thing, or act like he has a contract with
a machine. Instead, he should honor this animal and treat him
as an equal partner. Out of this understanding come many great
obligations for the rider, and the rider must be able to meet these
obligations. He has to be able to maintain his horse in the required
environment with all the little and big things attached.

—*Klaus Balkenhol, quoted in* Dressage Masters,
by David Collins

POLO

A polo handicap is a person's ticket to the world.

—*Sir Winston Churchill*

The money.

—*Answer by polo great Tommy Hitchcock to a newspaperman's question about what went first in polo: the horse or the player's knees, back, legs, reflexes, etc.*

One would-be assassin leaped suddenly in front of Spain's King Alphonso XIII's horse as he was riding back from a parade and pointed a revolver at the king from barely a yard away. "Polo comes in very handy on these occasions," said Alfonso afterward. "I set my horse's head straight at him and rode into him as he fired."

—*Source unknown*

Playing polo is like trying to play golf during an earthquake.

—*Sylvester Stallone*

She's a wonder at getting away,
And give her a length on the grass,
They can bid a good-day to the swift little bay,
For there's nothing can catch her or pass;
She fights for her head to the ball,
For the ponies are fond of the fun,
And oh! but she loves to be leading them all,
Does Witchery—fourteen-one.

—*Author unknown, "Witchery"*

Polo is a disease for which the only cure is money.

—*Source unknown*

Now a polo-pony is like a poet. If he is born with a love for the game he can be made. The Maltese Cat knew that bamboos grew solely in order that polo-balls might be turned from their roots, that grain was given to ponies to keep them in hard condition, and that ponies were shod to prevent them slipping on a turn. But, besides all these things, he knew every trick and device of the finest game of the world, and for two seasons he had been teaching the others all he knew or guessed.

—*Rudyard Kipling, "The Maltese Cat"*

RODEO

Rodeo cowboys usually keep goin' until they're crippled—injured by animals—run out of money for entry fees and traveling expenses, quit or get killed in the arena. The camaraderie among them is unlike any other sport.

—*Chris LeDoux*

The rodeo ain't over till the bull riders ride.

—*Ralph Carpenter*

~

Anyone who has ever experienced the thrill of rodeo life wishes it could go on forever. To remain healthy, strong, and capable. To keep going down the road never giving a thought as to when it all might end. But we are finite creatures, only given a short time in life to live our dreams.

—*Ralph Clark*

~

Be prepared to spend several months of your life in plaster of Paris.

—*Larry Mahan [advice to aspiring rodeo riders]*

~

Life is a catch pen full of rodeo broncs, and way I figure it, forty-six years into this buck-out, the mission is to decide, early on, Did you come to hide or did you come to ride? If the latter, it doesn't take too many seasons forked to this buckin' horse orb named Earth before we learn the crude rude truth of the old adage: Never a pony couldn't be rode, never a cowboy couldn't be thrown. And subordinating this proverb is yet another cowpoke dictum: Get pitched off, climb right back on. Rodeo, like Poetry, can get into your hemoglobin, into the deep helices of DNA, and once there, it becomes your metaphorical makeup for life.

—Paul Zarzyski, "Good Horsekeeping"

RACING

It is not best that we all think alike; it is difference of opinion that makes horse races.

—Mark Twain

When you peel back the layers of racing, you are left with the horse and the groom.

—Charlsie Canty

One way to stop a runaway horse is to bet on him.

—*Source unknown*

The first favourite was never heard of, the second favourite was never seen after the distance post, all the ten-to-oners were in the rear, and a dark horse which had never been thought of, and which the careless St. James had never even observed in the list, rushed past the grand stand in sweeping triumph.

—*Benjamin Disraeli*, The Young Duke *[this quotation marks the origin of the phrase "dark horse," meaning a long-shot]*

A racehorse is an animal that can take several thousand people for a ride at the same time.

—*Source unknown*

There are fools, damn fools, and those who remount in
a steeplechase.

—Bill Whitbread

You have to remember that about seventy percent of the horses
running don't want to win. Horses are like people. Everybody
doesn't have the aggressiveness or ambition to knock himself out
to become a success.

—Eddie Arcaro

The utter joy of riding Template lay in the immense power which
he generated. There was no need to make the best of things, on his
back; to fiddle and scramble, and to hope for others to blunder, and
find nothing to spare for a finish. He had enough reserve strength for
his jockey to be able to carve up the race as he wishes, and there was
nothing in racing, I thought, more ecstatic than that.

—Dick Francis, Nerve

People make a lot of fuss about the so-called heroic courage of jump jockeys, which is nonsense. We all know the risks and we accept them. Nothing can match the thrill of riding good horses at speed over fences—nothing! I don't see that courage has anything to do with it. It's simply a job we all enjoy doing.

—*Bob Champion, winner of the Grand National*

[Sunday Silence, winner of the 1989 Kentucky Derby] seemed to be some kind of prehistoric throwback, a living legend of the days when horses were hunted, when fear and hunger ruled their lives. In a classy stable of calm, earnest animals, Sunday Silence was Al Capone singing in the Vienna Boys Choir.

—*Jay Hovdey, Wittingham,* The Story of a Thoroughbred Legend

The harrowing uncertainty of the turf.

—*Red Smith*

The race is not always to the swift nor the battle to the strong—but that's the way to bet.

—Damon Runyan

Horses have never hurt anyone yet, except when they bet on them.

—Stuart Cloete

If this bureau had a prayer for use around horse parks, it would go something like this: Lead us not among bleeding-hearts to whom horses are cute or sweet or adorable, and deliver us from horse-lovers. Amen. . . . With that established, let's talk about the death of Seabiscuit the other night. It isn't mawkish to say, there was a racehorse, a horse that gave race fans as much pleasure as any that ever lived and one that will be remembered as long and as warmly.

—Red Smith

Secretariat was an amiable, gentlemanly colt, with a poised and playful nature that at times made him seem as much a pet as the stable dog was. I was standing in front of his stall one morning, writing, when he reached out, grabbed my notebook in his teeth and sank back inside, looking to see what I would do. "Give the man his notebook back!" yelled [Eddie] Sweat. As the groom dipped under the webbing, Secretariat dropped the notebook on the bed of straw.

Another time, after raking the shed, Sweat leaned the handle of the rake against the stall webbing and turned to walk away. Secretariat seized the handle in his mouth and began pushing and pulling it across the floor. "Look at him rakin' the shed!" cried Sweat. All up and down the barn, laughter fluttered like the pigeons in the stable eaves as the colt did a passable imitation of his own groom.

—*William Nack*, Pure Heart

I'll be around as long as horses think I'm smarter than they are.

—*Trainer James E. "Sunny Jim" Fitzsimmons*
[who continued to train horses into his nineties]

Now a barrier looms, dark and menacing, in your path. You feel an almost imperceptible change in your horse's momentum as he adjusts his stride to meet the takeoff point. You tighten your legs against his sides to give encouragement in the last few critical strides. Your body picks up the horse's emphatic rhythm, and you feel the great hindquarters gather under you. Suddenly, you are in the air, feeling the clean, exhilarating sensation of a flight.

You are on a 'chaser.

—*Raymond Woolfe, Jr.*, Steeplechasing

No one has ever bet enough on a winning horse.

—*Richard Sasuly*

You're better off betting on a horse than betting on a man. A horse may not be able to hold you tight, but he doesn't wanna wander from the stable at night.

—*Betty Grable*

The only sport I'm not interested in is horse racing. That's because I don't know the horses personally.

—*Nat King Cole*

A horse gallops with his lungs, perseveres with his heart, and wins with his character.

—*Federico Tesio*

It can be set down in four words: the best of everything. The best hay, oats and water.

—*James ("Sunny Jim") Fitzsimmons, Thoroughbred racehorse trainer, on how to train winning horses*

Breed the best to the best, and hope for the best.

—*Traditional breeding advice*

You can eat your betting money, but never bet your eating money.
—Sign in many racetrack cafeterias

Betting the ponies is done in various methodical ways by professionals, haphazardly by some enthusiasts, and often in a rather bizarre fashion by others just out for a day's lark.
—Cooky McClung, Horsefolk Are Different

I think that boxing and horse racing are the sports that probably produce the greatest characters. Part of the reason is that in both sports, no matter where you turn, the scent of larceny is in the air. That's a very sweet odor that lends itself to characters and funny situations.
—Dick Schaap

A hoss is a gen'leman, kid. It hurts him to lose a race, it breaks him—
permanent—to see a race.
—*Lincoln Steffans*, The Autobiography of Lincoln Steffans

The first time he saw Seabiscuit, the colt was walking through
the fog at five in the morning. Smith would say later that the horse
looked right through him. As if to say, "What the hell are you
looking at? Who do you think you are?" He was a small horse,
barely fifteen hands. He was hurting too. There was a limp in his
walk, a wheezing when he breathed. Smith didn't pay attention to
that. He was looking the horse in the eye.
—*Narrator, in the film* Seabiscuit

But if we offer prizes for races with ridden horses—young and
half-grown colts as well as full-grown beasts—we shall be cultivating
a sport well in keeping with the nature of our territory.
—*Plato*, Laws VIII

"Races are won with that seat, sir."

"Be damned to that," said my uncle Valentine. "If the horse is good enough, he'll win with the rider facing his tail."

—*Donn Byrne, "Destiny Bay"*

There are a hundred ways to lose a race, but only one way to win one.

—*Racing maxim*

The more you know, the more you win. That is the allure of horse race handicapping.

—*Charles Carroll*, Handicapping Speed

Losers walking around with money in their pockets are always dangerous, not to be trusted. Some horse always reaches out and grabs them.

—*Bill Barich*, Laughing in the Hills

Horse racing is animated roulette.
                    —*Roger Kahn, "Intellectuals and Scholars,"*
                                        The American Scholar

Most good horses know when they'd won: filled their lungs and
raised their heads with pride. Some were definitely depressed when
they lost. Guilt they never felt, nor shame nor regret nor compassion.
                                        —*Dick Francis*, Break In

Politics is like a racehorse. A good jockey must know how to fall
with the least possible danger.

                                                —*Edouard Herriott*

[Steeplechasing] is one of the real sports that's left, isn't it? A bit
of danger, a bit of excitement and the horses—the best thing in
the world.

                            —*Queen Elizabeth, the Queen Mother*

You can take an old mule and run him and feed him and train him and get him in the best shape of his life, but you ain't going to win the Kentucky Derby!

—*Pepper Martin*

You're never a superhorse until you're retired. Any horse can be beaten on any given day.

—*Angel Cordero, Jr., jockey*

Each handicap is like a hurdle in a steeplechase, and when you ride up to it, if you throw your heart over, the horse will go along, too.

—*Laurence Bixby*

According to the best traditions, sunrise on a spring morning is supposed to make a guy glad to be alive. But at sunrise, how can a guy tell he's alive? There is a law in the benighted state of New York which bars children from racetracks in the afternoon, the archaic theory being that frequenting a gambling hell is an occasion of sin for minors. Wherefore a small boy, if he is to be reared properly, must be taken to the track for the morning works.

—*Red Smith, "Clockers Are Little Men"*
in The Red Smith Reader

The fires burnt high in him. He should have lived with the wild horses of the prairie where he could have been boss. There the issue would have been settled quickly; he would have ruled or died. But civilization got him instead. Man laid hold of his bridle. "All right," said Display, "you asked for it," and he gave it to them. Finally he did what they asked but not because he had changed his mind.

—*J. A. Estes, on the Thoroughbred racehorse Display*

Horses and jockeys mature earler than people—which is why horses are admitted to racetracks at the age of two, and jockeys before they are old enough to shave.

—*Dick Beddoes*

Don't fall off.

—*Advice given by Hollie Hughes, an elderly trainer of thoroughbred race horses to Secretariat's jockey Ron Turcotte before the 1973 Belmont Stakes (which Secretariat went on to win by 33 lengths)*

If you could call the thing a horse. If it hadn't shown a flash of speed in the straight, it would have gotten mixed up with the next race.

—*P. G. Wodehouse,* Very Good, Jeeves

I feel as a horse must feel when the beautiful cup is given
to the jockey.
>   —*Edgar Degas, on seeing one of his paintings sold at auction*

Out on the Texas plains a fellow had to be a smart horseman to win a
race and a smarter one to win a bet—and collect it!
>   —*Samuel Clay Hildreth,* The Spell of the Turf,
>   *quoted in* The Colonial Quarter Race Horse
>   *by Alexander Mackay-Smith*

There appears to be no immunity to this dangerous germ. If as
a parent you observe your little precious pick up a toy horse, make
galloping noises, and plop it over a block, screaming "Win!" you've
had it. The jumping rider's disease is loose in your house.
>   —*Raymond Woolfe, Jr.,* Steeplechasing

I bought five more horses [after John Henry, 1981 and 1984
Horse of the Year]. Two are with the Canadian mounted police.
One's directing traffic out on Union Avenue. One is up at Cornell:
they can't figure out if it's a male or female. And a last one a friend
bought for $5,000 to spare me further embarassment.

>   —*Sam Rubin, quoted in* They're Off! Horse
>   Racing at Saratoga *by Edward Hotaling*

I know nothing about racing, and any money I put on a horse is
a sort of insurance policy to prevent it winning.

>   —*Frank Richardson*

There's no sense in whipping a tired horse, because he'll quit on you.
More horses are whipped out of the money than into it.

>   —*Eddie Arcaro*

It is Australian innocence to love the naturally excessive and be
proud of a thoroughbred bay gelding who ran fast.
　　　　—Peter Porter, "Phar Lap in the Melbourne Museum"

You talk of riders on the flat, of nerve and pluck and pace—
Not one in fifty has the nerve to ride a steeplechase.
It's right enough, while horses pull and take their faces strong,
To rush a flier to the front and bring the field along;
Bur what about the last half-mile, with horses blown and beat—
When every jump means all you know to keep him on his feet.
When any slip means sudden death—with wife and child to keep—
It needs some nerve to draw the whip and flog him at the leap.
　　　　—Andrew Barton "Banjo" Paterson, "Tommy Corrigan"

A trainer can always find an excuse for a defeat, whether it's a mistake in judgment by the jockey or the conditions of the track or a bit of poor racing luck. Maybe just a little adjustment—a new rider or a change in equipment or a different post position—will make the next outcome different. "This is the great thing about racing," trainer D. Wayne Lucas once said. "There's always another race."
—*Billy Reed*, Thoroughbred: A Celebration of the Breed

HUNTING

Twas the sound of his horn called me from my bed,
And the cry of his hounds has me oft-times led,
For Peel's View-halloo would waken the dead,
Or a fox from his lair in the morning.
—*John Woodcock Graves*, "John Peel"

What a fine hunting day, it's as balmy as May,
When the hounds to our village did come.
Every friend will be there, and all troubles and care
Will be left far behind them at home.
See servants and steeds on their way
And sportsmen in scarlet display.
Let us join the glad throng that goes laughing along
And we'll all go a-hunting today.
[Chorus] So we'll all go a-hunting today
All nature looks smiling and gay;
Let us join the glad throng
That goes laughing along
And we'll all go a-hunting today.

— *"And We'll All Go Hunting Today"*

When half the drowsy world's a-bed
And misty morning rises red,
With jollity of horn and lusty cheer,
Young Nimrod urges on his dwindling rout;
Along the yellowing coverts we can hear
His horse's hoofs thud hither and about:
In mulberry coat he rides and makes
Huge clamour in the sultry brakes.

—Siegfried Sassoon, "Nimrod in September"

Apart from the crowd with its banter and mirth,
Sitting loose on his mare with an eye to the whins,
He has looked to his curb, he has tightened his girth,
He has marked out a place where the big double thins.
Here's a good one to follow,
To follow, to follow—
A good one to follow when business begins.

—Will H. Ogilvie, "The Man to Follow"

Here's to the fox in his earth below the rocks!
And here's to the line that we follow,
And here's to the hound with his nose upon the ground,
Though merrily we whoop and we hollow.

Then drink puppy drink, and let every puppy drink
That is old enough to lap and to swallow;
For he'll grow into a hound, so we'll pass the bottle 'round,
And merrily we'll whoop and we'll hollow.

—"Drink Puppy Drink"

Then he was aware of Mustard-Pot gathering himself as though
to clear the moon, of the tow-path dropping away, of brown
water scurrying under, of brown water leaping up, of a bombshell
splash that flung white fountains high and high above his drowning
eyes, and of a Force, a Force enormous and earthquake-like under
his thighs, driving him up and up through the desperate waters.
Then the fountains subsided; and Lomondham knew himself still
in the saddle, knew his horse swimming like a swordfish to be in
at the death.

—Gilbert Frankau, "Mustard-Pot Matchmaker"

The worst of doing a big thing out hunting is the fact that in nine cases out of ten they who don't do it are as well off as they who do. If there were any penalty for riding round, or any mark given to those who had ridden straight—so that justice might in some sort be done—it would perhaps be better. When you have nearly broken your neck to get to hounds, or made your horse exert himself beyond his proper power, and then find yourself, within three minutes, over-taking the hindmost ruck of horsemen on a road because of some iniquitous turn that the fox has taken, the feeling is not pleasant. And some man who has not ridden at all, who never did ride at all, will ask you where you have been; and his smile will give you the lie in your teeth if you make any attempt to explain the facts. Let it be sufficient for you at such a moment to feel that you are not ashamed of yourself. Self-respect will support a man even in such misery as this.

—*Anthony Trollope,* The Eustace Diamonds

It ain't the 'unting as 'urts 'un, it's the 'ammer, 'ammer, 'ammer along the 'ard, 'igh ground.

—Punch *magazine cartoon caption*

The Galloping Squire to the saddle has got,
While the dewdrop is melting in gems on the thorn,
From the kennel he's drafted the pick of his lot,
How they swarm to his cheer! How they fly to his horn!
Like harriers turning or chasing like fire,
"I can trust 'em, each hound!" says the Galloping Squire.
                  —*G. J. Whyte-Melville, "The Galloping Squire"*

The first Marchioness [of Salisbury] was painted by Sir Joshua
Reynolds, and hunted till the day she died at eighty-five, when,
half-blind and strapped to the saddle, she was accompanied by
a groom who would shout, when her horse approached a fence,
"Jump, dammit, my Lady, jump!"
                  —*Barbara Tuchman,* The Proud Tower

The difference between a good jump and a bad jump is like the difference between playing in tune and playing out of tune—even a little bit off is awful. But in hunting there is the compensation, the wonderful compensation, of practicality: jumping over fences has the genuine purpose of getting from here to there. After years of brooding darkly over my imperfect days in the saddle (that is, all of them) I in realism adopted the binary system for rating my jumps. Forget the Olympic ten-point form scale; mine was one or zero—either I made it to the other side and was still in the saddle or I did not. (The time I got over and then immediately fell off into a pond I secretly scored as a two.)

—Stephen Budiansky

When good men ride in front of you,
And women most of all;
Ride with some little courtesy,
And give them room to fall.
To jump upon a sportsman
Displays a want of taste;
And killing large subscribers,
Is simply wanton waste.

—Anonymous, "Give Them Room"

I saw the hounds occasionally, sometimes pouring over a green bank,
as the charging breaker lifts and flings itself, sometimes driving
across a field, as the white tongues of foam slide racing over the sand;
and always ahead of me was Flurry Knox, going as a man goes who
knows his country, who knows his horse, and whose heart is wholly
and absolutely in the right place.

—*Somerville and Ross, "Phillipa's Fox Hunt,"*
Experiences of an Irish R. M.

Remember that the most important gait of the hunter is the halt.

—*William P. Wadsworth, M.F.H.,* Riding to Hounds
in America: An Introduction for Foxhunters

We are in for a gallop—away! away!
I told them my beauty could fly;
And we'll lead them a dance ere they catch us today,
For we mean it, my lass and I!
She skims the fences, she scours the plain,
Like a creature winged, I swear,
With snort and strain, on the yielding rein;
For I'm bound to humour the mare.

—*G. J. Whyte-Melville, "The Good Grey Mare"*

Women who ride, as a rule, ride better than men. They, the women, have always been instructed; whereas men have usually come to ride without any instruction. They are put upon ponies when they are all boys, and put themselves upon their fathers' horses as they become hobbledehoys: and thus they obtain the power of sticking on to the animal while he gallops and jumps,—and even while he kicks and shies; and, so progressing, they achieve an amount of horsemanship which answers the purposes of life. But they do not acquire the art of riding with exactness, as women do, and rarely have such hands as a woman has on a horse's mouth. The consequence of this is that women fall less often than men, and the field is not often thrown into the horror which would arise were a lady known to be in a ditch with a horse lying on her.

—*Anthony Trollope*, Hunting Sketches,
"The Lady Who Rides To Hounds"

The acme of bliss when you're hunting the fox
Is riding a horse who will jump off his hocks;
While quite the worst feeling, and one to be banned,
Is a horse which will only jump off his fore-hand.

—*Beatrice Holden, "Drop Your Hands"*

A fox-hunt to a foreigner is strange;
'Tis also subject to the double danger
Of tumbling first, and having in exchange
Some pleasant jesting at the awkward stranger:
But Juan had been early taught to range
The wilds, as doth an Arab turn'd avenger,
So that his horse, or charger, hunter, hack,
Knew that he had a rider on his back.

And now in this new field, with some applause,
He clear'd hedge, ditch, and double post, and rail,
And never craned, and made but few "faux pas,"
And only fretted when the scent 'gan fail.
He broke, 'tis true, some statutes of the laws
Of hunting—for the sagest youth is frail;
Rode o'er the hounds, it may be, now and then,
And once o'er several country gentlemen.

—*Lord Byron, "Don Juan"*

Two gentlemen met, both unhors'd, in a lane
(Foxhunting on foot is but labour in vain)
"Have you seen a brown horse?" "No, indeed, Sir; but pray,
In the course of your ramble have you seen a Grey?"
                    —*R. R. Egerton Warburton, "Two Gentlemen"*

He all the country could outrun,
Could leave both man and horse behind;
And often, ere the chase was done,
He reeled, and was stone-blind.
                    —*William Wordsworth, "Simon Lee, The Old Huntsman"*

Today, all day, I rode upon the down,
With hounds and horsemen, a brave company . . .
And once, when check'd, a thrush sang, and my horse
Prick'd his quick ears as to a sound unknown.
. . . Your face my quarry was. For it I rode,
My horse a thing of wings, myself a god.
                    —*Wilfrid Scawen Blunt, "St. Valentine's Day"*

There are only two classes of good society in England; the equestrian classes and the neurotic classes. It isn't mere convention; everybody can see that the people who hunt are the right people and the people who don't are the wrong ones.

—*George Bernard Shaw*, Heartbreak House

I've a head like a violin-case; I've a jaw like a piece of steel;
I've a mouth like India-rubber, and devil a bit I feel;
So I've had my fun with a biped thing that clambered upon my back,
And I'm in at the death, though I'm panting for breath,
right bang in the midst of the pack.

With a cockney sportsman mounted on top,
That has hired me out for the day,
It's the moment for me to be off for a spree
In a new and original way.
In my own most original way.
Oats! but my spirits were gay!
When I betted my bit that my rider should sit
Somewhere else ere the close of the day.

—*Anonymous*, "Bolts"

The British public who do not hunt believe too much in the jumping of those who do. It is thought by many among the laity that the hunting man is always in the air, making clear flights over five-barred gates, six-foot walls, and double posts and rails,—at none of which would the average hunting man any more think of riding than he would at a small house. . . . And here, in England, history, that nursing mother of fiction, has given hunting men honours which they here never fairly earned. The traditional five-barred gate is, as a rule, used by hunting men as it was intended to be used by the world at large; that is to say, they open it; and the double posts and rails which look so very pretty in the sporting pictures, are thought to be very ugly things whenever an idea of riding at them presents itself.

—*Anthony Trollope,* Hunting Sketches,
"The Man Who Hunts and Never Jumps"

The hunting season had come to an end, and the Mullets had not succeeded in selling the Brogue. There had been a kind of tradition in the family for the past three or four years, a sort of fatalistic hope, that the Brogue would find a purchaser before the hunting was over; but seasons came and went without anything happening to justify such ill-founded optimism. The animal had been named Berserker in the earlier stages of its career; it had been rechristened the Brogue later on, in recognition of the fact that, once acquired, it was extremely difficult to get rid of. The unkinder wits of the neighbourhood had been known to suggest that the first letter of its name was superfluous.

—*H. H. Munro (Saki)*, The Brogue

One of those game old things, whether they are old colonels who insist on wearing tight waists in their seventies, or old horses. . . . I say, he was one of those game old things that make a virtue of looking fit even when they might be excused drooping their heads and lying down to die.

—*Liam O'Flaherty, "The Old Hunter"*

When you've ridden a four-year-old half of the day
And, foam to the fetlock, they lead him away,
With a sigh of contentment you watch him depart
While you tighten the girths on the horse of your heart . . .
To you who ride young ones half-schooled and half-broke,
What joy to find freedom a while from your yoke!
What bliss to be launched with the luck of the start
On the old one, the proved one, the horse of your heart !
        —*Will H. Ogilvie, "The Horse of Your Heart"*

You gentlemen of high renown come listen unto me,
That take delight in foxhunting in every high degree.
A story true to you I'll tell concerning of a fox
Of Royston Hills and mountains high and over stony rocks.

Old Reynold being in his den and hearing of these hounds
Which made him for to prick his ears and tread upon the ground;
Methinks me hears some jubal hounds pressing upon my life
Before that they to me shall come I'll tread upon the ground.
        — *"The Foxhunt"*

Nearer, were twigs knocked into kindling,
A much bashed fence still dropping stick,
Flung clods, still quivering from the kick,
Cut hoof-marks pale in cheesy clay, The horse-smell
     blowing clean away.
The hunt has been, and found, and gone.

—*John Masefield, "Reynard the Fox"*

What a grand thing 'twould be if I could go
Back to the kennels now and take my hounds
For summer exercise; be riding out
With forty couple when the quiet skies
Are streaked with sunrise, and the silly birds
Grown hoarse with singing; cobwebs on the furze
Up on the hill, and all the country strange,
With no one stirring; and the horses fresh,
Sniffing the air I'll never breathe again.

—*Sigfried Sassoon*, The Old Huntsman

So when the long last day is done, and life's last covert's drawn;
When Gabriel turns his phantom steed and sadly sounds his horn;
There's just one thing I'll ask of Fate—
And that's for my chesnut horse to wait
To carry me over the Golden Gate
On Resurrection morn.

—*Dalesman, "The Bean"*

VI

SAYINGS

AND

NEIGHINGS

Proverbs, Equine Metaphors, and Other Notable Remarks

In one respect a cavalry charge is very much like ordinary life. So long as you are all right, firmly in the saddle, your horse in hand and well armed, lots of enemies will give you a wide berth. But as soon as you have lost a stirrup, have a rein cut, have dropped your weapon, are wounded, or your horse is wounded, then is the moment that from all quarters enemies rush upon you.

—*Winston S. Churchill, "Sensations of a Cavalry Charge"*

Words are as beautiful as wild horses, and sometimes as difficult to corral.

—*Ted Berkman*

As the traveler who has lost his way, throws his reins on his horse's neck, and trusts to the instinct of the animal to find his road, so must we do with the divine animal who carries us through this world.

—*Ralph Waldo Emerson*

He had got inside the very soul of the poor beast and taken me with him. I could not refrain from remarking: "I say, Leo Nikolayevich, beyond any doubt, you must have been a horse once yourself."

—*Ivan Turgenv, commenting on watching Leo Tolstoy whisper to an old horse*

A man who rode good horses was usually a good man.

—*Western expression, quoted in* They Rode Good Horses *by Don Hedgpeth*

The day was as hot as the sun on a bay horse's back.

—*Verlyn Klinkenborg, "Gratitude: When Contentedness Comes Home"*

Imagination is a good horse to carry you over the ground—not a flying carpet to set you free from improbability.

—*Robertson Davies,* The Manticore

Life is too short to ride bad horses.

—*Source unknown*

There is no need of spurs when a horse is running away.

—*Publicus Syrus*, Moral Sayings

How can anyone bear to put a horse—a horse that he loves—
at risk? Well, a horse doesn't live a full life just munching grass in
a field. Horses themselves seek excitement. I have put a horse at risk,
many times, and it has brought me great joy. If the horse had died,
I would never have forgiven myself. The horsey sports have this
contradiction at their very heart. Me, I asked the horse, and she
wanted to go. More than me.

—*Simon Barnes*

I've been kicked, stepped on and bitten. Bitten I liked least. My most trustworthy saddle horse leaned over once while I was cinching him up and clamped on my upper leg, turning the thigh into what looked like a Central American sunset. I threw him down on the ground, half-hitched his feet together, and put the tarp over him. I let him up two hours later; he thought I was the greatest man in the world, one he wouldn't think of biting. Horses only remember the end of the story.

—*Thomas McGuane, "Roping, from A to B"*

Or if we rode, perhaps she *did*
Pull sharply at the curb;
But the way in which she slid
From horseback was superb!

—*C. S. Calverley*

When a harvester grows weary of his work, it is said "He has the fatigue of the Horse." The first sheaf, called the "Cross of the Horse," is placed on a cross of boxwood in the barn, and the youngest horse on the farm must tread on it.

—*Sir James Frazer*, The Golden Bough

Never were abilities so much below mediocrity so well rewarded; no, not when Caligula's horse was made Consul.
　　—*John Randolph, regarding Richard Rush's appointment as Secretary of the Treasury [the mad emperor Caligula appointed his horse Incitatus a consul of Rome]*

A mule is just like horse, but even more so.
　　　　　　　　　　　　　　　　　　　　　—*Pat Parelli*

The same philosophy is a good horse in the stable, but an errant jade on a journey.
　　　　　—*Oliver Goldsmith, "The Good Natured Man"*

Time is the rider that breaks youth.
　　　　　　　　　—*George Herbert,* Jacula Prudentum

Like the pilgrims heading to Canterbury, we [trail riders] assemble at trailheads, tack up our horses while chattering with kindred spirits, then head out with eyes wide and ears at the ready. Our mode of travel allows interaction with nature unadulterated by the smelly cacophony of internal combustion engines. We hear the trickling brook, the songbirds, the bugle of an elk. The sound of hoofbeats and the occasional whinny of a horse complement the scene instead of destroying it.

— *Dan Aadland*, The Complete Trail Horse

He that will venture nothing must not get on horseback.

— *C. J. Apperley ("Nimrod")*, Quarterly Review

Organization is the art of getting men to repond like thoroughbreds. When you cluck to a thoroughbred, he gives you all the speed and strength of heart and sinew he has in him. When you cluck to a jack-ass, he kicks.

— *C. R. House*

The human mind is not rich enough to drive many horses abreast and wants one general scheme, under which it strives to bring everything.

—*George Santayana*

Science is not a sacred cow. Science is a horse. Don't worship it. Feed it.

—*Aubrey Eben*

All you need for happiness is a good gun, a good horse, and a good wife.

—*Daniel Boone*

It is not enough for a man to know how to ride; he must know how to fall.

—*Mexican proverb*

Is it possible, at certain moments we cannot imagine, a horse can add its sufferings together—the non-stop jerks and jabs that are its daily life—and turn them into grief? What use is grief to a horse?

—*Peter Shaffer,* Equus

The wagon rests in winter, the sleigh in summer, the horse never.

—*Yiddish Proverb*

No ride is ever the last one. No horse is ever the last one you will have. Somehow there will always be other horses, other places to ride them.

—*Monica Dickens,* Talking of Horses

In buying a horse or taking a wife, shut your eyes tight and commend yourself to God.

—*Tuscan Proverb*

The only time some people work like a horse is when the boss rides them.

—*Gabriel Heater*

Behold, he shall come up as clouds, and his chariots shall be as a whirlwind: his horses are swifter than eagles. Woe unto us! for we are spoiled.

—*Jeremiah* 4:13

The snorting of his horses was heard from Dan: the whole land trembled at the sound of the neighing of his strong ones; for they are come, and have devoured the land, and all that is in it; the city, and those that dwell therein.

—*Jeremiah* 8:16

Behold, we put bits in the horses' mouths, that they may obey us; and we turn about their whole body.

—*James* 3:3

The horse is prepared against the day of battle: but safety is
of the Lord.

—Proverbs 21:31

The horse is God's gift to man.

—Arabian proverb

The soul is like a pair of winged horses and a charioteer joined in
natural union.

—Plato

Show me your horse and I will tell you who you are.

—English proverb

Dog lovers hate to clean out kennels. Horse lovers like cleaning stables.

—*Monica Dickens*, Talking of Horses

To ride a horse well, you have to know it as well as you know your best friend.

—*Katie Monahan Prudent*

Men, my dear, are very queer animals, a mixture of horse-nervousness, ass-stubbornness, and camel-malice—with an angel bobbing about unexpectedly like the apple in the posset, and when they can do exactly as they please, they are very hard to drive.

—*T. H. Huxley*

There are instances when we are like horses, we psychologists, and grow restless: we see our own shadow wavering up and down before us.

—Friedrich Nietzsche

If a mule gets a leg caught in a barbed-wire fence, she will either figure out how to free herself without injury or will wait stoically and patiently for help. The mule rarely overeats to the point of detriment or drinks too much when overheated. A horse veterinarian once told me that if everyone rode mules she would soon be out of business.

—John Hauer, The Natural Superiority of Mules

There has to be a woman, but not much of a one. A good horse is much more important.

—Max Brand, on Western novels

I'm hostile to men, I'm hostile to women, I'm hostile to cats, to poor cockroaches, I'm afraid of horses.

—*Norman Mailer*

A cavalryman took the utmost pains with his charger. As long as the war lasted, he looked upon him as his fellow-helper in all emergencies and fed him carefully with hay and corn. But when the war was over, he only allowed him chaff to eat and made him carry heavy loads of wood, subjecting him to much slavish drudgery and ill-treatment. War was again proclaimed, however, and when the trumpet summoned him to his standard, the cavalryman put on his charger its military trappings, and mounted, being clad in his heavy coat of mail.

The horse fell down under the weight, no longer equal to the burden, and said to his master, "You must now go to the war on foot, for you have transformed me from a horse into an ass, and how can you expect that I can again turn in a moment from an ass to a horse?"

Moral: Damage is slow to mend.

—Aesop's Fables, *"The Horse and His Rider"*

Your head and your heart . . . keep up!
Your hands and your heels . . . keep down!
Your knees press into your horse's sides,
Your elbows into your own!

—English proverb

Every horse is good for something.

—Tom Smith, in the film Seabiscuit

A mule will labor ten years willingly and patiently for you, for the privilege of kicking you once.

—William Faulkner

Mules will test your horsemanship. You must be patient, kind, gentle, consistent and very persuasive in order to train mules and get along well with them. They separate the "men from the boys" when it comes to horse training. This is one of the reasons that I am a mule fan.

—*Robert M. Miller, DVM*

There is no secret so close as that between a rider and his horse.

—*Robert Smith Surtees,* Mr. Sponge's Sporting Tour

The riders in a race do not stop short when they reach the goal. There is a little finishing canter before they come to a standstill. . . . The canter that brings you to a standstill need not be only coming to rest. It cannot be while you still live.

—*Supreme Court Justice Oliver Wendell Holmes, Jr., reflecting on retirement in a radio address on his ninetieth birthday*

The punters know that the horse named Morality rarely gets past the post, whereas the nag named Self-Interest always runs a good race.

—*Gough Whitlam*

The sun it was, ye glittering gods, ye took to make a horse.

—*Dirga-Tamas*

You will find it is always easier to walk if there is a horse between your legs.

—*Source unknown*

Old minds are like old horses; you must exercise them if you wish to keep them in working order.

—*John Adams, second president of the United States*

The stable wears out a horse more than the road does.

—*French proverb*

Horses leave hoofprints on your heart.

—*Source unknown*

Some people have animal eyes—bears' eyes, cats' eyes, pigs eyes—
but horses have human eyes and I love horses better than people.

—*Jose Garcia Villa*

Some things, of course, you can't change. Pretending that you have is
like painting stripes on a horse and hollering "Zebra!"

—*Eddie Cantor*

I would rather ride on an ass that carries me than a horse that throws me.

—George Herbert

Another man's horse and your own spurs outrun the wind.

—German proverb

God forgive you for galloping when trotting's not a sin.

—Scottish proverb

Betwixt the stirrup and the ground
Mercy I asked, mercy I found.

*—William Camden [epitaph for a man
killed by a fall from a horse]*

If you see a piebald horse, make a wish before you see his tail.

—Gypsy saying

A horse is a thing of such beauty . . . none will tire of looking at him as long as he displays himself in his splendor.

—Xenophon, On Horsemanship

It was yer hosses done likked us!

—Confederate soldier surrendering to First Vermont Cavalry, a unit mounted on Morgans

God first made Man. He thought better of it and made Woman. When He got time He made the Horse, which has the courage and spirit of Man and the beauty and grace of Woman.

—Brazilian saying

The difference between an author and a horse is that the horse
doesn't understand the horse dealer's language.

—*Max Frisch*

A foundered horse will oft debate
Before he tries a five barred gate . . .

—*Jonathan Swift*

The air of heaven is that which blows between a horse's ears.

—*Arabian proverb*

The lawyers—tell me why a hearse horse snickers hauling a
lawyer's bones.

—*Carl Sandburg, "The Lawyers Know Too Much"*

Up hill spare me;
Down hill forbear me;
Plain way, spare me not,
Let me not drink when I am hot.

—*English proverb*

Ride a cock-horse to Banbury Cross,
To see a fine lady upon a white horse;
With rings on her fingers and bells on her toes
She shall have music wherever she goes.
—*Nursey rhyme [the "fine lady" refers to Queen Elizabeth I who traveled to the town of Banbury to see a stone cross erected there]*

. . . This most noble beast is the most beautiful, the swiftest and of the highest courage of domesticated animals. His long mane and tail adorn and beautify him. He is of a fiery temperament, but good tempered, obedient, docile and well-mannered.
—*Pedro Garcia Conde, 1685*

Gypsy gold does not chink and glitter. It gleams in the sun and neighs in the dark.

—Gypsy saying

There is something about riding down the street on a prancing horse that makes you feel like something, even when you ain't a thing.

—Will Rogers

Every horse thinks his own pack the heaviest.

—Anonymous

[Fate is] a little like a horse with a loose rein. It can meander calmly, or break into a gallop without warning, leaving you to hang on for dear life.

—Star Trek: The Next Generation

Speak your mind, but ride a fast horse.

—*Anonymous*

Because we have the best hay and the best oats and the best horses.
—*Colonel Sir Harry Llewellyn, Passports to Life
[recalling his answer when asked why the British show
jumping team was so successful in the 1952 Olympics]*

I really like his character. If he was a person now, he'd be my
best friend.
—*Grand prix rider Ian Millar, talking about his horse Big Ben*

And God took a handful of southerly wind, blew His breath over it
and created the horse.

—*Bedouin legend*

A Hibernian sage once wrote that there are three things a man
never forgets: The girl of his early youth, a devoted teacher, and
a great horse.

—*C. J. J. Mullen*

A good horse makes short miles.

—*George Eliot*

A horse's behavior will be in direct proportion to the number of
people watching you ride him.

—*Cooky McClung*

The wildest colts make the best horses.

—*Plutarch*

The spirited horse, which will try to win the race of its own accord, will run even faster if encouraged.

—*Ovid*

Ride the horse in the direction that it's going.

—*Werner Erhard*

You never know how a horse will pull until you hook him to a heavy load.

—*Paul Bryant*

She who waits for her knight must remember—she will have to clean up after his horse.

—*Source unknown*

A fine little smooth horse colt,
Should move a man as much as doth a son.

—Thomas Kyd

One can't shoe a running horse.

—Dutch proverb

Courage is being scared to death and saddling up anyways.

—John Wayne

We judge a horse not only by its pace on a racecourse, but also by its walk, nay, when resting in its stable.

—Michel de Montaigne

He that hath love in his heart hath spurs in his sides.

—English proverb

I have just read your dispatch about sore tongued and fatigued sick horses. Will you pardon me for asking what the horses of your army have done since the battle of Antietem that fatigues anything?

—Abraham Lincoln, letter to Gen. George B. McClellan

Horses and poets should be fed, not overfed.

—Charles II of England

We kept him until he died . . . and sat with him during the long last minutes when a horse comes closest to seeming human.

—C. J. J. Mullen

Never give up. For fifty years they said the horse was through.
Now look at him—a status symbol.

—*Fletcher Knebel*

The wind flew. God told the wind to condense itself and out of the
flurry came the horse. But with the spark of spirit the horse flew by
the wind itself.

—*Marguarite Henry*, King of the Wind

A horse already knows how to be a horse; the rider has to learn how
to become a rider. A horse without a rider is still a horse; a rider
without a horse is no longer a rider.

—*Source unknown*

We all want everything to be wonderful. Every woman wants to sit upon a horse dressed in bells and go riding off through the boundless green and sensual forest.

—*Clarissa Estes,* Women Who Run with the Wolves

In grateful and reverent memory of the Empire's horses (some 375,000) who fell in the Great War (1914–1918). Most obediently, and often most painfully, they died.

—*Memorial at Church of St. Jude, London*

To be loved by a horse, or by any animal, should fill us with awe—for we have not deserved it.

—*Marion Garretty*

For what the horse does under compulsion, as Simon also observes, is done without understanding; and there is no beauty in it either, any more than if one should whip and spur a dancer.

—*Xenophon*

Sell the cow, buy the sheep, but never be without the horse.

—*Irish proverb*

No one can teach riding so well as a horse.

—*C. S. Lewis*

The only constant thing in life is change, and things can change rapidly when you're dealing with horses.

—*Pat Parelli*

A fool and his horse are soon parted.

—*Source unknown*

Spring and summer are riding on a piebald mare.

—*Russian proverb*

There are times when you can trust a horse, times when you can't, and times when you have to.

—*Source unknown*

The horse loves his oats more than his saddle.

—*Russian proverb*

An old friend is like a saddled horse.

—*Afghanistani proverb*

Nature has not placed us in an inferior rank to men, no more than the females of other animals, where we see no distinction of capacity, though I am persuaded if there was a commonwealth of rational horses . . . it would be an established maxim amongst them that a mare could not be taught to pace.

—*Mary Wortley*

We are like horses who hurt themselves as soon as they pull on their bits—and we bow our heads. We even lose consciousness of the situation, we just submit. Any re-awakening of thought is then painful.

—*Simone Weil*

Once a horse is born, someone will be found to ride it.

—*Hebrew proverb*

Raise your horse as a son, ride him as an enemy.

—*Arabian proverb*

All I say is, nobody has any business to go around looking like a horse and behaving as if it were all right. You don't catch horses going around looking like people, do you?

—*Dorothy Parker*

I have not permitted myself, gentlemen, to conclude that I am the best man in the country; but I am reminded, in this connection, of a story of an old Dutch farmer who remarked to a companion once that "it was not best to swap horses while crossing streams."

—*Abraham Lincoln*

A man sentenced to death obtained a reprieve by assuring the king he would teach his majesty's horse to fly within the year—on the condition that if he didn't succeed, he would be put to death at the end of the year. "Within a year," the man explained later, "the king may die, or I may die, or the horse may die. Furthermore, in a year, who knows? Maybe the horse will learn to fly." My philosophy is like that man's. I take the long-range view.

—*Bernard Baruch*

But America is a great, unwieldy Body. Its Progress must be slow. . . . The fleetest Sailors must wait for the dullest and slowest. Like a Coach and six—the swiftest Horses must be slackened and the slowest quickened, that all may keep an even Pace.

—*John Adams*

I find the Englishman to be him of all men who stands firmest in his shoes. They have in themselves what they value in their horses, mettle and bottom. Mettle: spirited; bottom: capacity to endure strain.

—*Ralph Waldo Emerson*

Reckless automobile driving arouses the suspicion that much of the horse sense of the good old days was possessed by the horse.

—*Source unknown*

A horse's eye disquiets me: it has an expression of alarm that may at any moment be translated into action.

—*E. V. Lucas*

Quality is like buying oats. If you want nice, clean, fresh oats, you must pay a fair price. However, if you can be satisfied with oats that have already been through the horse . . . that comes a little cheaper.

—Source unknown

One must plow with the horses one has.

—German proverb

What the colt learns in youth he continues in old age.

—French proverb

Most nations, free ones especially, should be dealt with like a spirited horse, whom a judicious rider will keep steady, by maintaining an exact balance in his seat, showing neither fear nor cruelty, occasionally giving and checking with the rein, while he prudently and resolutely corrects with the spur, or kindly blandishes with his hand.

—*Francis Gentleman, "A Trip to the Moon"*

Care, and not fine stables, makes a good horse.

—*Danish proverb*

No philosophers so thoroughly comprehend us as dogs and horses.

—*Herman Melville*

Who buys a horse buys care.

—*Spanish proverb*

A little neglect may breed mischief: for want of a nail the shoe was lost; for want of a shoe the horse was lost; and for want of a horse the rider was lost.

—*Benjamin Franklin,* Poor Richard's Almanac
[*also found in* Jacula Prudentum *by George Herbert*]

Few girls are as well shaped as a good horse.

—*Hannah Arendt*

If time were the wicked sheriff in a horse opera, I'd pay for riding lessons and take his gun away.

—*W. H. Auden*

We ought to do good to others as simply as a horse runs, or a bee makes honey, or a vine bears grapes season after season without thinking of the grapes it has borne.

—*Marcus Aurelius*

So, I can tell when the horse is right because I spent eighteen years on, not horses, but spaceships and spacesuits.

—*Alan Bean*

Some people regard private enterprise as a predatory tiger to be shot. Others look on it as a cow they can milk. Not enough people see it as a healthy horse, pulling a sturdy wagon.

—*Winston Churchill*

When my horse is running good, I don't stop to give him sugar.

—*Doug Horton*

A catcher and his body are like the outlaw and his horse. He's got to ride that nag till it drops.

—*Johnny Bench*

If you ride a horse, sit close and tight,
If you ride a man, sit easy and light.
                    —*Benjamin Franklin*, Poor Richard's Almanack

He that riseth late, must trot all day, and shall scarce overtake his business at night.
                    —*Benjamin Franklin*, Poor Richard's Almanack

The child who is fortunate enough to be associated with horses during his formative years can look back on fond memories, and those who continue to ride, hunt, or show during their lifetime seldom experience anything more gratifying than the thrill of winning their first ribbon.

—*Stephen O. Hawkins, in* Learning to Ride, Hunt, and Show, Gordon Wright

The horse is both intelligent enough and stupid enough to do what we demand of him.

—*George Gaylord Simpson*, Horses

While there are many things you can fake through in this life, pretending that you know horses when you don't isn't one of them.

—*Cooky McClung*, Horsefolk Are Different

Of all creatures, the horse is the noblest.
> —*Gervase Markham*, The Compleat Horseman

For the student there is, in its season, no better place than the saddle.
> —*Francis Parkman*, Autobiography

Fat is the best color.

> —*Horseman's adage*

You sometimes hear the old saying "Fat is the best color." This means, of course, that fat covers a multitude of conformation faults and therefore looks good—especially to the less discerning horseman.
> —*Eleanor F. Prince and Gaydell M. Collier*, Basic Horse Care

Watching a seasoned pony carry its young rider, one senses the pony is doing the teaching. With an uncanny sense of the rider's limitations and often genuine kindness, ponies seem to possess an intelligence you don't always see in horses.

—Nina Duran, A Pony Rider's Diary

Animals do not admire each other. A horse does not admire its companion.

—Thomas Mann

You have to bear in mind that Mr. Autry's favorite horse was named Champion. He ain't ever had one called Runner Up.

—Gene Mauch, manager of the Los Angeles Angels, owned by Gene Autry

A horse never runs so fast as when he has other horses to catch up
and outpace.

—Ovid

The will is a beast of burden. If God mounts it, it wishes and goes
as God wills; if Satan mounts it, it wishes and goes as Satan wills;
Nor can it choose its rider . . . the riders contend for its possession.

—Martin Luther

It's hard to lead a cavalry charge if you think you look funny
on a horse.

—Adlai E. Stevenson

I made over forty Westerns. I used to lie awake nights trying to think
up new ways of getting on and off a horse.

—William Wyler

Let us put Germany in the saddle, so to speak—it already knows how to ride.

—*Otto von Bismarck, in a speech to the German Reichstag*

Some of my best leading men have been dogs and horses.

—*Elizabeth Taylor*

Words are as beautiful as wild horses, and sometimes as difficult to corral.

—*Ted Berkman, in* The Christian Science Monitor

Human reason is like a drunken man on horseback; set it up on one side and it tumbles over on the other.

—*Martin Luther*

Not the fastest horse can catch a word spoken in anger.

—*Chinese proverb*

A good resolution is like an old horse: often saddled but
rarely ridden.

—*Mexican proverb*

Competitions are for horses, not for artists.

—*Attributed to composer Bela Bartok*

Of all Creatures God made at the Creation, there is none except man
more excellent, or so much to be respected as a Horse.

—*Bedouin proverb*

A horse shoe that clatters needs a nail.

—*Spanish Proverb*

Ride a cow until you ride a horse.

—*Japanese proverb [meaning: make do with what you can get until something better comes along]*

Hurry! At a gallop! To Paradise!

—*The last words of Madame Louise, daughter of Louis XV of France*

To finish is to win.

—*Endurance riding motto*

I speak Spanish to God, Italian to women, French to men and
German to my horse.

—*Charles V, Holy Roman Emperor*

A nod is as good as a wink to a blind horse.

—*Irish proverb*

One must get off one's horse over its head; to step off is merely weak.
—*Mao Tse-Tung*

[The horse possesses] a singular body and a noble spirit, the
principle thereof is a loving and dutiful inclination to the service
of Man, wherein he never faileth in Peace nor War . . . and therefore
. . . we must needs account it the most noble and necessary of all
four-footed Beasts.
—*Edward Topsel, quoted in* Horsewatching, *by Desmond Morris*

To be an equestrian in the classical sense is not to be just a rider. It is a position in life. It is a stance we take in relation to life. We must make a choice between self-love, the promotion of our own well-being of our ego, and love for the horse. That is the fundamental attitudinal decision that earned Xenophon the title Father of Classical Dressage: he dared to love a horse!

> —*Charles de Kunffy*, Training Strategies
> for Dressage Riders

Never threaten to take away a kid's horse, unless you don't care if they start trusting horses more than you. If a young person is having or causing trouble, the horse may be their salvation.

> —*Lesli K. Groves, "Kids & Horses: Rated PG-17,"*
> *in* America's Horse *magazine*

Don't ride the high horse. The fall, when it comes, is hard.

> —*American proverb*

The American Saddle Horse, with his refinement of gaits and his animation and beauty, does not belong just to his owner or trainer. He belongs to the show ring, where he can bring joy and thrill to thousands of "ringside riders."

—*Marguerite Henry*, Album of Horses

The speed of a runaway horse counts for nothing.

—*Jean Cocteau, artist*

Soft grass for an old horse.

—*Bulgarian proverb*

Polo is a disease for which poverty is the only cure.

—*Source unknown*

The substitution of the internal combustion engine for the horse marked a very gloomy milestone in the progress of mankind.

—Sir Winston Churchill

~

For centuries we have been famed for our skill in horsemanship, so that the Magyar has no need to have his horses dance with crossed legs, Spanish fashion.

—King Mathias I Corvinus of Hungary, to his father-in-law, the King of Naples, who had sent him a Spanish riding master

~

The Budweiser Clydesdales! I'm so glad to see you. Now that John Wayne and Elvis are gone, you're all we have left!

—CB message from a driver who saw the vans pulling the Budweiser Clydesdales (quoted in All the King's Horses, *by Alix Coleman and Steven D. Price)*

~

My horse be swift in flight even like a bird,
My horse be swift in flight.
Bear me now in safety far from the enemy's arrows.
And you shall be rewarded with streamers and ribbons red.

—Sioux warrior's song to his horse

The horse that pulls the most is usually given the least amount
of oats.

—German proverb

I haven't been able to ride very much since my hip operation several
years ago. I think I would still be playing polo if I hadn't had that. If I
ever got to where I couldn't ride, I don't think I'd live very long.

*—Cecil Smith (generally considered to have been America's
most outstanding polo player. He played his last polo game
at age eighty-three and last rode at ninety-three)*

Equestrian art, however, is something else which involves complete harmony between horse and rider, and that makes the rider feel that there have been moments of beauty and greatness which make a flight possible from all that is ordinary and mediocre.

—*Nuno Oliveira*, Notes and Reminiscences
of a Portuguese Rider

One reason why birds and horses are not unhappy is because they are not trying to impress other birds and horses.

—*Dale Carnegie*, How to Win Friends
and Influence People

With horses and warriors, you can't judge from their appearance.

—*Japanese proverb*

Put the horse before the cart.

—*English proverb*

No horseman or horsewoman has ever finished learning.
—*Mary Gordon-Watson*, The Handbook of Riding

A wise horse cares not how fast a man may run.
—*Armenian proverb*

If the horse is good, you don't mind paying the rental fee.
—*Japanese proverb*

The empire was won on horseback, but you cannot govern
on horseback.
—*Chinese general Yeh-lu T'su T'sai, quoted in Anthony Dent,*
The Horse Through Fifty Centuries of Civilization

Old horses for young riders, old riders for young horses.

—*Horseman's proverb*

Nature will never disclose all her secrets to us, and the horse will forever have in store for us novelties, surprises, springing from life itself.

—*General Alexis L'Hotte*, Questions Equestres, *quoted in Jean Froissard*, Equitation: Learning and Teaching

Horses are karmic and they come to us in our lives karmically, when it is time for us truly to learn.

—*Dominique Barbier, with Mary Daniels*, Dressage for the New Age

In order to go fast, one must go slow.

—*Horseman's proverb*

Do not mistake a goat's beard for a fine stallion's tail.

—Irish proverb

There is a natural affinity between women and horses, something
so basic it creates an immediate foundation for a relationship and a
launching pas for almost everything we want to do with a horse.

—Mary D. Midkiff, Fitness, Performance
and the Female Equestrian

One white foot—buy him,
Two white feet—try him;
Three white feet—look well about him,
Four white feet—go without him.

—Old horse-buying prejudice

Tell it to the Horse Marines

—*Old saying*

War is no place for horses.
—*British show jumping rider and horse show organizer*
Colonel Sir Mike Ansell, Soldier On

Never change horses in midstream.

—*Old adage*

A mule is an animal that has neither pride of ancestry nor hope of posterity.

—*Source unknown*

For bringing us the horse we could almost forgive you for bringing us whiskey. Horses make a landscape more beautiful.

—*Lame Deer, quoted in Alice Walker,*
Horses Make a Landscape More Beautiful

Heretofore, every peasant knew only too well that when he had a horse he could manage his homestead and that without a horse he could not make a living. . . .

—*Nikita Khrushchev, in a speech to*
the Communist Party Congress

When the horse dies, dismount.

—*Anonymous*

Talking to a horse's ear.

—*Japanese expression (meaning to say*
something that falls on deaf ears)

But a horse is a labor of love as well as a responsibility, an aesthetic as well as a dynamic pleasure, something to contemplate as well as to ride.

—Sarah Montague, in Nina Duran, A Rider's Diary

Horses are something to dream about . . . and to wish for; fun to watch . . . and to make friends with; nice to pat . . . and great to hug; and, oh, what a joy to ride!

—Dorothy Henderson Pinch, Happy Horsemanship

The slow horse reaches the mill.

—Irish proverb

It's difficult to water a horse that won't lower its head.

—Finnish proverb

Straight from the horse's mouth.

—*Old expression*

Put a beggar on horseback and he'll ride to hell.

and

Put a beggar on horseback and he'll go on a gallop.

—*Irish proverbs*

When I hear somebody talk about a horse or a cow being stupid,
I figure it's a sure sign that animal has outfoxed them.

—*Tom Dorance*

Stable thinking is the ability to say "neigh."

—*Source unknown*

An old horse finds its way best.

—*Norwegian proverb*

All King Edward's Horses Canter Many Big Fences.

—*Mnemonic for the A-K-E-H-C-M-B-F
letters around a dressage arena*

A loose horse will always be found at the barn.

—*Indian proverb*

You can lead a horse to water . . . if you got a horse.

—*English proverb*

The first horse to drink doesn't get dirty water.

—Nigerian proverb

Dead horses don't kick.

—Bulgarian proverb

The horse's death makes the cow fatter.

—English proverb

A bad foaling might still produce a fine horse.

—French proverb

Folk songs? They're all folk songs—I never heard a horse sing.
                    —*Louis "Sachmo" Armstrong [also attributed*
                             to folk singer Woody Guthrie]

When the mule is beaten, the horse is scared.
                                              —*Chinese proverb*

There is no greater pleasure than a nice ride on a nice horse on a beautiful day.
                              —*Judy Richter,* Pony Talk

May your descendants ride in chariots.
                                   —*Chinese good luck wish*

The horse is, like man, the most beautiful and the most miserable
of creatures.

—*Rosa Bonheur*

Horses have hoofs to carry them over frost and snow; hair, to protect
them from wind and cold. They eat grass and drink water, and fling
up their heels over the campaign. Such is the real nature of horses.
Palatial dwellings are of no use to them.

—*Chunang Tzu*

Men are not hanged for stealing horses, but that horses may not
be stolen.

—*George Savile, Marquess of Halifax*, Reflections

A donkey appears to me like a horse translated into Dutch.

—*Georg Christoph Lichtenberg*

It is not the duty of the horse to be a biofeedback mechanism for yearning humans; yet it is remarkable how consistently people with horses claimed to have learned much about themselves through them. Certainly, the management of a horse will give you a rapid evaluation of your patience, your powers of concentration, and your ability to hold on to delicate ideas for sustained periods of time.

—*Tom McGuane*, Some Horses

From a workaday drudge, [the Shetland pony] became a fun-loving playmate. No door was closed to him, for he had taught himself how to slide bolts, open gates, rattle latches. His long lips became expert at plucking caps from children's heads or handkerchiefs from pockets.

—*Marguerite Henry*, Album of Horses

Being born in a stable does not make a man a horse.

—*Arthur Wellseley, Duke of Wellington [on learning he had been described as Irish because he had been born in Dublin]*

Lend a horse, and you may have back his skin.

—*English proverb*

⁓

The primeval instincts of the horse are nowhere more pronounced than in the bond between the mare and her foal, for the maternal instinct is the strongest in nature. It is this instinct that ensures the survival of the species and determines the character of the mare and her attitude toward other horses and toward man.

—*Hans-Heinrich Isenbart*, The Beauty of the Horse

⁓

Men are better when riding, more just and more understanding, and more alert and more at ease and more under-taking, and better knowing of all countries and all passages. . . .

—*Edward, Duke of York*

⁓

Reason lies between the spur and the bridle.

—*George Herbert*, Jacula Prudentum

Never gallop Pegasus to death.

—*Alexander Pope, "Epistle I, Prologue*
to the Imitations of Horace"

I have thought that to breed a noble horse is to share with God in one of His mysteries, as well as one of His delights.

—*Tom Lea*, The Hands of Cantu

A horse is worth more than riches.

—*Spanish proverb*

INDEX